London Transport
Bus Garages

John Aldridge

Ian Allan
PUBLISHING

Contents

Introduction 3

1. Garage development 4

2. Garages closed before privatisation 21

3. Garages used by London Buses
   or former London Buses companies after privatisation 76

   Arriva London North/North East 76
   Arriva London South 86
   East Thames 92
   First CentreWest 94
   London Central 100
   London General 105
   London United 113
   Metroline 124
   Metroline London Northern 131
   Stagecoach East London 134
   Stagecoach Selkent 141
   The Original London Sightseeing Tour 144

4. Non-London Buses operators of LT routes 145

Index 157

First published 2001

ISBN 0 7110 2812 5

© Ian Allan Publishing Ltd 2001

Published by Ian Allan Publishing

an imprint of Ian Allan Publishing Ltd, Hersham, Surrey KT12 4RG.
Printed by Ian Allan Printing Ltd, Hersham, Surrey KT12 4RG.

Code: 0112/B

Cover:
Mortlake was one of London's oldest garages, dating back to horse-bus days. This view was taken on a Sunday, hence the numerous parked Routemasters. But just visible at the back are two RTs (one green) used for training duties and temporarily hired through the London Bus Preservation Group in 1978. *Geoff Rixon*

Title page:
By contrast, Waterloo represents current thinking (or economics), with virtually all its fleet stabled in the open and roofing provided only for areas where work such as maintenance is undertaken. *Author*

Introduction

Much has changed since the original book with this title was published in the 1980s. The privatisation from the early 1990s of the bus-operating side of London Transport means that, with one exception, the only garages owned by London Buses or, more accurately, its master, Transport for London, are those surplus to requirements at the time of privatisation but which for various reasons have not been sold off. The exception is Ash Grove, which is now partly used by TfL's own subsidiary, East Thames Buses, though another operator uses the yard.

These developments have dictated major changes to the format of this edition. The first chapter looks at the design and development of the London bus garage over almost 100 years. The second lists depots and garages (including those for trams and trolleybuses) which were in use after World War 2 but which have subsequently closed.

Chapter 3 lists the major bus-operating companies that emerged with privatisation, and the garages or yards from which they operated at that time. The list also includes premises which have been acquired subsequently, as well as any which are temporarily mothballed or which have since been vacated.

The smaller operators and most newcomers to London often work from fairly basic yards, though there are some notable exceptions. A few of those listed have since become part of larger groups, such as Grey-Green

(now part of Arriva) and Capital Citybus (now part of FirstGroup), but logic dictates that they appear in Chapter 4.

One long-lasting feature of London bus operation has been the use of one- or two-letter codes, displayed on the sides of the vehicles, to denote the garage from which they are operating. While the names of some of the garages are easily identifiable (eg FW — Fulwell), others (such as AD — Palmers Green) are by no means obvious, albeit well known to older enthusiasts, at least. Unfortunately not all the privatised operators have continued to display them, though most have. Indeed, many have used London-style codes for premises acquired more recently. However, it has recently emerged that London Transport / Transport for London has itself devised what can best be described as 'shadow' codes to identify new operators or premises, and in some cases these differ from the operator's own code. For example, Arriva London South's Beddington Farm depot in Croydon was known to the operator as BF but to LT/TfL as CN; Arriva is itself now adopting the shadow code. For completeness and simplicity, therefore, the book includes two indices to individual garages. One lists them in alphabetical order of the obvious name of the location, commencing with Abbey Wood, the other in order of garage code, starting (unsurprisingly!) with A — Sutton. The latter includes both TfL (marked with an asterisk) and operator codes.

Above:
'Which one's ours?' A crew stands in Hounslow garage in 1953 looking for the right bus among the RTs on five different routes. *Geoff Rixon*

Garage development

The London Passenger Transport Board had a well-deserved reputation for good design and architecture, particularly with its new tube stations. Its new bus garages of the 1930s were of a similarly high standard, but unfortunately — so far as this book is concerned — most were in the LPTB's Country Area, and outside the scope of this narrative. Many of the inherited premises in the Country Area were of poor quality and traffic was growing there quite fast, so the early emphasis was well away from Central London. The number of new Central Area bus garages or trolleybus depots built was small. Just one of the latter was constructed; all the others were adapted and improved tram depots. New Central Area bus garages were not numerous either, there being just three, of which only one survives.

Ironically, the major post-World War 2 programme to build new garages was again focussed mainly on the Country Area, where New Towns were to make a particular impact. Indeed, the one and only example of

the LTE's ideal garage was the Country Area one at Garston, near Watford; most of the others built were regarded as slight compromises, mainly because site layout was a limiting factor. Most money for garages in what might be termed the 'red bus' area went mainly into adapting or replacing former tram and (later) trolleybus depots. Few new Central Area bus garages were constructed in the 1950s or 1960s. There were exceptions, such as North Street, Romford, a very necessary garage that did not replace any but which was intended to relieve the hard-pressed Hornchurch (RD) garage in coping with traffic to a new London County Council estate. Peckham (PM) was another new garage to reduce pressure elsewhere, but all the others replaced former tram depots. Ironically, within a few years provision here proved to be over-generous.

The long-lasting bus strike of 1958 did permanent harm to passenger numbers, which were already declining with the increase in private motoring and the

Below:
Alperton was one of three Central Area garages built by the LPTB in the 1930s and is the only one remaining. In this 1940 picture passed by the censor, bomb damage visible on the left has resulted in road traffic being diverted through the garage. The new 'prewar' RTs inside the garage are in temporary storage until brake problems have been solved. Note the elaborate lamp over the garage entrance. *Author's collection*

Above:
LT's postwar garages were again designed to a high standard. This is North Street, Romford, precisely named to distinguish it from the Green Line garage in the town. Note the tower with LT roundel over the staircase. *Gerald Mead*

impact of television. That led to a period of retrenchment in which the size of the fleet fell by about 15%, and inevitably garage closures followed. Even in trolleybus days, some of the depots had spare space which in the 1950s was often used to store surplus buses.

It was not until well into the 1970s that any kind of garage-building programme was again given serious consideration, and by then it was a very expensive business, costing £5 million or more (at 1980 prices) per garage. Another irony is that some of these expensive new buildings, with their high standards of construction and amenity for both staff and buses, were to be closed in the early days of route tendering and the run-up to privatisation of the red bus fleet. Ash Grove, Streatham and others came and went, while older ones such as Kingston hung on (by a thread) for several more years.

The round of closures began before London tendering, but followed placement of the red buses under the wing of the Greater London Council (as the LCC had become). That had come about in 1970, when Country Area buses and coaches were hived off to the National Bus Company. Loss of tenders for routes running into or entirely within Essex resulted in closure of Loughton (L), itself a postwar garage.

After privatisation, or even in the run-up to it, the newly formed 'red bus' companies were hard-up for cash. Not only could they generally not afford new buses; they also had to look closely at how much use they were making of the garage space they had. A half-empty garage, as, for example, Victoria (GM) had become, imposed an enormous burden on the business as a whole, and in particular on the economics of the remaining fleet based there. The short-term nature of those early route contracts, usually of two or three years,

did not encourage or even permit long-term planning. There is little difference in the overhead costs of the half-full garage compared to a full one.

Some of the winners of tenders in the early days incurred considerable dead-mileage costs in working buses and drivers to and from a route operated from a relatively remote depot. For example, London & Country won route 293 (Epsom–Morden) in 1986 and proceeded to work it from its Dorking garage, while more recently London & Country, later Arriva, ran route 85 (Kingston–Putney Bridge) from Leatherhead garage, until the lease on that garage was terminated at short notice. Over in Essex, Blue Triangle has successfully run a number of routes in Central and even South London, admittedly on a short-term basis, with buses and drivers coming from Rainham.

Tellings-Golden Miller ran several tendered routes from Byfleet, Surrey, for some years before finding accommodation nearer the main focus of its operations. That accommodation is at Fulwell (FW), once a tram depot and more recently a trolleybus one, and now and for some time a garage of London United. This shared garage is a new concept, though the two parts are totally separate, and TGM has a separate address. But London United would have liked the extra space at Fulwell, which had previously been used by the London Bus Sales Department. Another example of a shared garage is at Edgware (EW), where both Sovereign and Metroline have parts, Metroline previously having used only the yard outside. The third example is a recent development at Ash Grove (AG), which only reopened in 2000 and which supports TfL's own (and only directly-owned) operation, East Thames Buses. But over in the yard are buses of another operator, Hackney

5

Community Transport, now trading on its London tendered routes as CT Plus. Inside Ash Grove garage itself is another surprise, for, though it is one of the most modern depots in London, some of the offices are housed in portable buildings. Apparently the existing offices would have needed quite a deal of work to bring them up to a reasonable standard.

Portable buildings are a feature at several recent depots — one can hardly call them garages, though in the old days London buses had garages, while trams and trolley-buses had depots. London generally is probably old-fashioned in that a fair proportion of the bigger fleets are kept under cover overnight. But in the UK generally, open-air or mainly open-air garages have been becoming more common for years, even in such cold locations as Inverness. London did carry out one experiment on these lines at an East London garage in the 1930s, but though the start of the experiment was publicised, nothing was apparently ever said about the result.

London persisted for a long time in building garages with a fair proportion of covered space. It also went on building garages to a far higher standard (and hence cost) than what became the norm elsewhere. Some 40 years ago a director of British Electric Traction, then one of the country's three leading bus-operating groups, told me that he had calculated one of his new covered garages, complete with pits and other accommodation, cost half as much as the London equivalent. About the only example of a predominantly open-air London depot is the one at Waterloo, which was converted from a bus stand relatively recently despite considerable opposition from the local council and residents of flats bordering the site. But there is now a possibility that it may revert to its former use.

Once route tendering got underway, for newcomers the difficulty of finding at any economic rent any suitable space for parking and servicing buses meant that open-air yards with amenities (such as they were) in portable buildings were usually the only choice. Portable buildings also have an advantage in that, not being permanent, they do not attract rates. Open sites are usually away from town centres and often in industrial estates, the quality and general *ambience* of which varies enormously. More recent examples are often titled 'business park' — a name suggesting a standard of appearance and amenity that is not always achieved. But at least such sites usually have

adequate parking space for cars too, and that is something all too often lacking at traditional garages in built-up areas.

Having said that, busmen do not necessarily work at or from the nearest garage to where they live. Victoria garage in its last days was notable in drawing its drivers and conductors from all over London. Many had gravitated there when their own local garage became entirely one-person-operated, and of course the free travel facilities they enjoy made such transfers a practical proposition. Recently, newcomer Connex Bus provided free travel on its trains, and that was undoubtedly an inducement to staff or potential staff living further out, even if its Beddington Lane, Croydon, base is not exactly near a railway station.

The area around Beddington Lane has become a honeypot for bus depots. First on the scene was London & Country with its new Beddington Farm depot — mainly open-air but built to a higher standard than most; it is now part of Arriva London South. Also in the area is Mitcham Belle, a well-established coach operator but a relative newcomer to London bus operation, though it now has four tendered routes; its original coach base at Mitcham doesn't have room for all the buses it now operates. Such a concentration in a relatively small area has disadvantages too; one potential operator of Croydon-area routes decided that staff recruitment and retention would be very difficult indeed and decided to look elsewhere altogether.

Even where there may apparently be suitable open space in London for a depot, there may be difficulties in getting planning permission. Travel London (part of the National Express Group) based its two London services at the Stewarts Lane, Battersea, depot of train operator Gatwick Express, a sister company. To the average observer that might seem a suitable additional use for a site already dedicated to transport interests, but local planners and residents thought otherwise and Travel London gave up, passing its routes to Limebourne.

Of course, even where operators have long-established premises there are often complaints, usually from locals living in houses built much more recently than the garage. But, usually, lack of suitable alternative facilities (and the threat of loss of local bus services) is sufficient to dissuade councils from taking drastic action.

Suitable location has always been a problem, partly because London has not always grown or spread in the way predicted. Even in the 1930s, when planning restrictions were few, developers did not always pursue their house-building as expected and there were quite often long runs to or from garages before taking up or finishing work on a route. That gave rise to the strange and unexplained phrase 'when working', which was a feature of many London bus tickets in the days when tickets were specific to each route. 'When working' meant when working to or from the garage to take up the running or finish on a particular route. Buses doing this used to carry passengers, whereas unfortunately today's new tendered-route environment does not allow this.

In those days wages were relatively low, though busmen were well paid, so garage journeys were not

regarded as too much of an expense. Old Kent Road (P) was one of London's more centrally-placed garages and over the years worked a surprising variety of routes, some quite distant. The opening of the new Victoria garage in 1940 was therefore quite a benefit to the fleet as a whole, which makes its recent closure seem strange. But one of the other disbenefits of route tendering is that individual routes have to be operated by one company (even if it uses more than one garage), and this has caused a number of well-established routes to be divided. Even where division has not taken place, dead or effectively dead mileage can be incurred when a garage is at one end of a route and vehicles have to be worked empty to the other end even though another operator may have a conveniently-located garage there.

But routes are probably more settled now, in terms of participating garage or garages, than used to be the case. In the 1920s and 1930s routes used to be altered and revised with surprising frequency. A chance to earn a bit more money here, or perhaps a small economy by going this way, led to a surprising lack of stability — something we all imagine is a recent phenomenon. Routes were often moved from garage to garage, and then perhaps back to where they were before, in almost bewildering fashion. From the mid-1950s onwards, when staff shortages started to bite, there were more moves but for a different reason; North West London was the biggest problem, so routes were partly switched to give garages elsewhere a bigger share of the work.

London also had an onerous union agreement that (with a few long-standing exceptions) crews would only work on one route in the course of a day's shift. As the number of hours worked per day dropped, and the five-day week came in, it became more and more difficult to get a worthwhile number of productive hours out of crews, and it became more important too as more routes became loss-making. Unfortunately the solution was to change the routes, particularly on Saturdays, and often again on Sundays, to the bewilderment of passengers. Changes were (and still are) inevitable in the process called localisation, which means replacing one route with two, hopefully with overlapping sections, to try and reduce the effects of traffic congestion. Other changes came about in the 1970s in particular with the introduction of more and more one-person operation, which sometimes meant leaving the busier part of the route worked by crewed buses, with the remainder (under a different number) operated by a one-person bus.

An integral part of the story about London's bus garages concerns not just the buildings themselves, of course, or their location, but also the types of buses they ran or still run and the routes on which they were used. While it is obviously impossible to mention all the types and changes, some of which occurred with bewildering frequency, some mention is made of some of the more interesting. Examples include Hendon garage (AE), with its prewar Leyland STDs, and Potters Bar (PB), with the one and only rear-engined Routemaster.

One habit of the 1920s and 1930s which seems strange is the way new buses would not infrequently be allocated to a garage and then (sometimes just a few months later) be taken away and replaced by much older vehicles. One might have thought, for example, that when the Metropolitan Police (which had considerable powers over London bus operation for many years) accepted the argument for covered-top double-deckers, following the experiment with four NSs, the route and garage in question would have kept them or even gained more. It didn't.

There can be very good reasons for changes in type allocation. In 1939 there was a big reshuffle, following many further conversions of petrol-engined buses to diesel, to try to give individual garages an all-petrol- or all-diesel-engined allocation. This was not just to avoid the wrong fuel being put into a vehicle but also to simplify fuel storage arrangements at the garage. Almost as soon as this had been done, the outbreak of World War 2 led to a further big reshuffle, coupled with reductions in services, to withdraw petrol-engined ST-type double-deckers wherever possible. This was partly because they had a lower seating capacity but also because the military at that time required petrol in large quantities rather than diesel fuel. But the cuts proved too severe, and quite a number of withdrawn STs were soon back on the road. As the war went on and transport needs became even more pressing, the neat type allocations loved by the engineers were often lost, and the situation subsequently worsened through the allocation of different types of utility buses.

Even so, standardisation at garages or groups of garages was still practised whenever possible, so that, for example, the big wartime fleet of utility Guy Arabs was based at relatively few garages. But part of the reason for this was that many Utilities were higher than traditional London buses and would not fit under the doorways at a number of garages. When production of the postwar RT family got underway, some of the allocations seemed surprising, with quite large numbers at some garages. But there were two particularly good reasons. One was that, in the early postwar era of shortages, there were only 12 servicing kits available for the first 520 postwar RTs delivered.

Above:
LT's policy of grouping garages so that major work was usually carried out by a parent garage in each group meant that when Hounslow was rebuilt its new steam-cleaning plant also cleaned the underside of buses from Turnham Green garage, as here. *Author*

The other was that, though the RT was relatively low in overall height at 14ft 3½in (most provincial buses were higher), it was slightly higher than an STL, and there were nearly 40 Central Area garages that could not accommodate RTs until the garage doorways (and occasionally the internal roof structure too) could be raised.

Something similar had had to take place when the first covered-top double-deckers came along in the late 1920s. Later, too, in the 1950s, there were numerous exchanges between garages of RTs (built by AEC) and RTLs (Leyland) to try to keep just one type in each engineering group: garages were grouped in small numbers with a parent in each group responsible for more major docking or heavier work. Changes around were not limited to the bus fleet, either: on 8 June 1949 there was a big reshuffle of many of the remaining trams between depots to allow the start of building work for replacement by buses, and further reshuffles followed later.

The closure of three garages in 1958, after the long bus strike that year, involved 750 bus movements and also the withdrawal of many RTLs, with many surplus buses being put into store; several bus garages were used for storage and a number of trolleybus depots were also utilised.

Above:
A traverser was usually provided in tram depots to avoid the need for a mass of pointwork. Here Abbey Wood's traverser is being used to move an RTL into position ready for its first day of bus operation. *Kevin Lane collection*

Below:
Less than 24 hours before the last picture was taken, trams spend their last night in an already partly demolished depot. *John Gillham*

Above:
Staff welfare was regarded as important from an early stage. This is Upton Park's canteen, complete with billiard tables, in the early 1930s. *Author's collection*

A feature of all the changes of motive power — from horse bus to motor bus, from tram to trolleybus or bus, and from trolleybus to motor bus — has been an interim period (intended to be short) at some depots when both forms of traction ran side-by-side from the same premises. The most bizarre, though not unique, must have been when the LGOC's chief motor-bus depot at Cricklewood also housed some 300 horses and their horse buses. Much later, the advent of World War 2 meant that two tram depots also ran trolleybuses alongside for several years, while the scenario was repeated some years later — but for months, not years — at a couple of trolleybus depots.

Finding sites for garages or depots has never been easy, though some operators say the present position is hopeless. Even in the 1930s, planning permission was not always forthcoming, but the LPTB was apparently willing to take a chance on occasions and buy suitable land in half-a-dozen different towns. In addition it then had nearly a dozen different places where garage building was intended, either for a new stand-alone garage or for a garage to replace one or more existing garages. Part of the plan included three new and large garages in Central London, at Marylebone, Pentonville and Victoria. Of these, only Victoria was ever built, on land acquired 10 years previously.

One garage that would have been closed too, though new, was at Potters Bar, which had proved too far north for the routes or traffic the garage had to handle; even in the 1930s it was judged that its location required an extra 20 bus crews. It is situated outside Greater London and in recent times has again been judged to be in the wrong place, but happily it has survived in operational use.

Another proposal was for a new garage at Mortlake (M), to replace not only the existing garage but also that at Twickenham (AB), though surprisingly there were also proposals to acquire land at nearby Richmond. In the event, and many years later, both Mortlake and Twickenham have closed, without direct replacement. In 1973 another look at garage requirements and deficiencies brought the promise of new garages at Hackney, Thamesmead and Westbourne Park. In addition there were to be improvements to Alperton (ON), Riverside (R), Streatham (AK) and Willesden (AC), while Seven Kings (AP) would be rebuilt.

Later in the 1970s there were agonising calculations over Mortlake, with Turnham Green / Chiswick (V) and Riverside also involved in the plans to end up with just two. This was at a time when LT was under the control of the Greater London Council and no longer the free agent it had been back in the 1930s to make its own decisions. Various scenarios were explored. Mortlake was hemmed in by housing and had a difficult entrance, could not accommodate even RMLs and was an old garage. Turnham Green suffered from being old, small and almost triangular in shape. Riverside (originally named Hammersmith) was cramped and badly laid out and also on a site to be redeveloped with better bus/tube interchange facilities.

Above:
Rather later decor features in this view of the canteen at New Cross, taken after its conversion to a bus garage.
Author's collection

By this time there was another factor important in any garage relocation: staff well-being and recruitment — something that had merited little consideration in the 1930s, though of course, in welfare matters generally, London busmen were better treated than most. Going back even further, after Colonel Searle, designer of the legendary B type, first became Chief Engineer of the LGOC, he decided to reallocate the incredibly mixed fleet to standardise on one type per garage. There were no 'ifs' or 'buts': the drivers moved with their buses. He recalled: 'The changes round had to take place after the buses had finished working at 12 o'clock at night. Stores had to be packed in buses, drivers' homes had to be changed, and transport had to be arranged for those drivers whose new homes still had to be found.' It must be remembered that, at that time, drivers would only have been trained or experienced on one or two types, and the characteristics and even controls of different makes would have varied considerably.

Back in 1977, what LT wanted to do was to close Mortlake and Turnham Green, modernise the former tram shed at Chiswick and build a new Riverside garage. Riverside would have been large — apparently the tenth largest in the fleet, with accommodation for 125 buses — and would also have taken over Mortlake's vehicles and staff. LT admitted that larger garages could be expected 'to give rise to management problems' but thought the trend to larger garages inevitable because they offered economies of size and, anyway, were necessary to house the new generation of buses which were larger.

Chiswick would have a capacity of 65 and was the key to the whole programme. Riverside garage was expected to cost £2.8 million, plus an extra £2 million for stronger foundations so that shops or offices could be built above. If and when approval for the new Riverside to go ahead was given by the GLC, then the first step would be to modernise Chiswick so that Riverside's allocation could temporarily move there. After it was built the buses and crews would return home and Mortlake and Turnham Green would both close, with their work moving to Chiswick. Reality turned out rather different, with Chiswick being modernised as a bus garage but all three of the others closed.

Of the other prewar proposals, two of the planned garages were ultimately built, in the early 1950s, at Peckham (PM) and Stockwell (SW), though the latter was for buses replacing trams rather than as an additional bus garage to relieve existing ones. As well as Gillingham Street, Victoria, mentioned earlier, the other two to be completed in the late 1930s were Alperton (ON) and Edgware (EW). Alperton was ready by mid-1939, initially gaining an allocation of diesel-engined STLs including some of the very latest. The third Central Area garage actually planned and built was Edgware, but Alperton is the only one surviving today. Edgware was overtaken by events, later becoming too small and being replaced quite recently by a larger building. This shows how difficult it has been, over the years, to predict future demand.

When the next comprehensive look at garage requirements was taken in the early postwar years, LT was still

Above:
In the late 1930s many busmen were enthusiastic members of the Territorial Army. Here personnel of the 260 and 261 Batteries of the 84th Anti-Aircraft Brigade (all LPTB employees) parade outside Stonebridge trolleybus depot before leaving for camp in Cornwall in August 1939.
Author's collection

struggling to cope with pent-up demand at a time of considerable vehicle shortage. The study listed some 25 garages with insufficient space, where buses were being parked in streets nearby (over 70 buses) or on nearby land (over 450 buses), but also noted that some 300 more buses were parked in the open at their garages. All told, some 10 garages were listed for rebuilding or for completely new development, with space for over 1,300 buses between them. Happily most of these schemes did come to pass, but three never saw the light of day. Walham Green (which presumably would have replaced Riverside) and King's Cross (presumably a substitute for the prewar Pentonville proposal) never happened, and Sidcup (SP) never was doubled in size. All these plans were for Central Buses as it was, as they were made before the tram and trolleybus organisation was brought into the new all-enveloping Central Road Services. The originally separate plans for tram replacement in South London listed seven depots to be rebuilt for bus use, plus two totally new ones, at Rye Lane, Peckham (RL) and Stockwell; the latter was originally conceived as an additional bus garage.

Moving on a decade or so and it was the turn of the trolleybus depots to be rebuilt for motor-bus use, and this was ultimately achieved by adapting the existing buildings, all except one of which had originally been tram depots. But four depots closed altogether — Colindale (CE), Ilford (ID), Isleworth (IH) and Lea Bridge (LB) — while a fifth — Hammersmith (HB) — was used instead to house the coaches owned by British European Airways which were operated on its behalf

by LT. The remaining 13 depots were all adapted for motor-bus operation. Trolleybus depots were generally more up-to-date in terms of facilities in that they had been modernised in the mid- to late 1930s, whereas the tram depots surviving after World War 2 were fairly original. Hopes for the future development of traffic were also more realistic when the trolleybus-to-motor-bus plans came along, and indeed from the outset there was rather more integration with existing bus routes and their garages. Even so, the need for economy and rationalisation soon caught up with a few of the former trolleybus depots; Carshalton (CN) lasted only five years with buses before closure.

From the late 1960s onwards there was a huge intake of long single-deckers as a big programme of converting routes to one-person operation got underway. The earliest examples were 36ft long — a dimension that soon proved difficult to accommodate on many London roads, later orders being for 33ft 5in versions, though

even these did not fit easily into some garages. Garages with their origins in horse-bus or early motor-bus days were a particular problem: Mortlake and Turnham Green have already been mentioned, but there were others where internal layouts were poor and amenities dated. Eventually a new programme of garage building was announced and indeed was carried through. When the new Uxbridge (UX) garage was opened in 1983 in replacement of a long-inadequate shed on the Denham Road outside the town, it was claimed to be the first brand-new garage for 29 years. That was an exaggeration, since Ash Grove (AG), replacing both Dalston (D) and Hackney (H), had opened in 1981, the same year as the new Plumstead (PD), replacing the old Plumstead (AM) and Abbey Wood (AW), and the new Westbourne Park (X), replacing both Stonebridge (SE) and Middle Row (X). More was to follow, with new garages at Norwood (N) and Streatham (AK), a major improvement at Norbiton (NB) and various other works.

Above:
In earlier days, when staff turnover was low and housing conditions were not so good, garage and depot life had a stronger social aspect. Here busmen at Merton garage queue for the 1937 pay-out from their Christmas Club. *Author's collection*

Ramifications of opening a new garage

Opening a new garage (which did not replace any other) at the Bull Yard, Peckham, set off an enormous reshuffle of route allocations designed to ease pressure on other garages. When it came into use on 2 May 1951 it took over route 36 (Hither Green–West Kilburn) from Catford and Camberwell garages and the Nunhead garage workings on route 78 (Shoreditch–Dulwich Library).

But there were also numerous consequential rearrangements. Since Catford was relieved of buses for the 36 it was able to take from Bromley some of its workings on route 47 (Farnborough–Shoreditch), which in turn allowed the transfer from Elmers End of the single-deckers on route 227 (Crystal Palace–Penge). Nunhead, relieved of its 78s, took over the buses formerly worked by Old Kent Road garage on the 173 (Peckham/Nunhead circular), and the latter was then able to take some of the route 4 (Finsbury Park–Bermondsey) buses previously worked by Holloway. That garage in turn accepted some of the 19s (Upper Tooting–Finsbury Park) from Battersea, while a further move was that of the 68A (Norwood Junction–Chalk Farm) from Norwood garage to Camberwell garage, balanced in part by the transfer of 195 (Stockwell–Norwood Garage) from Camberwell to Norwood garage. In terms of numbers Elmers End benefited most in losing 21 buses, which made it possible to cease parking some of its allocation on the forecourt of the local railway station.

Above:
An innovation in some trolleybus depots where turning space was limited, as at Hounslow (later renamed Isleworth),
was to put a turntable on the traverser so that vehicles could be turned round as well as moved to different parking lanes.
Author's collection

Above:
Rebuilding of garages whilst services continue to run has always been difficult.
Here building materials, STLs and RTs all mix at Hounslow garage in 1953. *Geoff Rixon*

Right:
The LGOC had taken bus garage design seriously since about 1912. This glazed pit with workshop area at the end is at the 'show' garage of Elmers End, built in 1929.
Author's collection

Far right
Visible in this view of part of the pit area of Stockwell garage (built in the early 1950s) are overhead rails and a hoist for lifting heavy components.
Author's collection

Below:
LT's standard postwar design was well thought out yet could be adapted to suit sites of varying shape: land availability and cost was an important factor. *Author's collection*

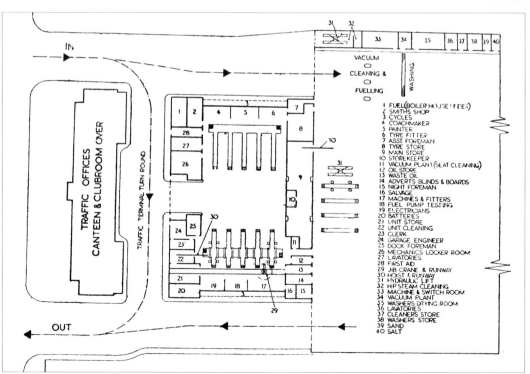

IN

OUT

TRAFFIC OFFICES
CANTEEN & CLUBROOM OVER

TRAFFIC TERMINAL TURN ROUND

VACUUM
CLEANING &
FUELLING

WASHING

1 FUEL (BOILER HOUSE UNDER)
2 SMITHS SHOP
3 CYCLES
4 COACHMAKER
5 PAINTER
6 TYRE FITTER
7 ASST FOREMAN
8 TYRE STORE
9 MAIN STORE
10 STOREKEEPER
11 VACUUM PLANT (SEAT CLEANING)
12 OIL STORE
13 WASTE OIL
14 ADVERTS BLINDS & BOARDS
15 NIGHT FOREMAN
16 SALVAGE
17 MACHINES & FITTERS
18 FUEL PUMP TESTING
19 ELECTRICIANS
20 BATTERIES
21 UNIT STORE
22 UNIT CLEANING
23 CLERK
24 GARAGE ENGINEER
25 DOCK FOREMAN
26 MECHANICS LOCKER ROOM
27 LAVATORIES
28 FIRST AID
29 JIB CRANE & RUNWAY
30 HOIST & RUNWAY
31 HYDRAULIC LIFT
32 HP STEAM CLEANING
33 MACHINE & SWITCH ROOM
34 VACUUM PLANT
35 WASHERS DRYING ROOM
36 LAVATORIES
37 CLEANERS STORE
38 WASHERS STORE
39 SAND
40 SALT

But, sadly, this was a turning point. Within a few years, garage closures — closures without replacement, that is — would become the norm as tendering slimmed down the size of the fleet. Worse, in the 1990s closures were to include some of these expensive new garages. Norbiton has vanished, Streatham is unused and Ash Grove has only recently reopened, but with an allocation a shadow of its former numbers.

Despite the arrival of several smaller operators, the majority of London routes are now operated by companies which are part of larger groups. But security of tenure on a route is only five years, with a possible extension to seven, and in such circumstances no group is likely to hazard, say, £6 million on a brand-new garage. The other side of the coin is that existing assets have to be fully utilised, or perhaps more than fully utilised; for example, First London's Westbourne Park garage had an initial allocation of 78 buses, but was said to have a capacity of slightly more than that; by 2001, with adjacent land rented from Railtrack, its allocation was an incredible 205 buses.

In the early years of motor-bus operation by the LGOC, it is unlikely that over-much thought was given to garage design, since the pressing problem was simply to find or build more accommodation for the growing fleet, and in the years up to 1914 one or two garages were even built by the LGOC's own staff. But, certainly from the 1920s, increasing attention was paid to the design and layout of garages, and by the middle of the decade the engineers had definite ideas on the subject. George Shave, the LGOC's Operating Manager and Chief

Engineer, thought a square shape the best and separate entrance and exit essential. A single-span roof was preferred, and there should be a generous forecourt or running-in area so that buses awaiting cleaning and fuelling did not obstruct the public highway. A roof height of 16ft would avoid any possible accident to anyone standing on top of an open-top double-decker. High-pressure hoses for washing would be hung from the roof, and the pits would all be linked at one end to a sunken workshop area. A simple overhead crane on tracks could be used for changing engines and gearboxes, and an overhead water-sprinkler system would guard against fire. The 'showpiece' or state-of-the-art garage exemplifying this approach was opened at Elmers End (ED) in 1929.

In appearance, bus garages are not particularly exciting places, but the LPTB went to enormous trouble to build attractive and durable tube stations in the 1930s and had a similar approach to bus garages it built, though sadly few still survive, and only the one in the Central Area — Alperton. But a similar tradition was followed in the 1950s, with some form of tower or higher point and an attractive frontage being used to clad what was basically a large shed behind. North Street, Romford (NS), opened in 1953, is an example. External bow-string supports rising above roof level were a feature of the new Shepherds Bush garage, opened in 1954, whilst both Peckham and Stockwell made use of reinforced-concrete barrel-vaulted roofs. That at Peckham was giving some cause for concern before the garage was pulled down a few years ago, but Stockwell's was and is

the more dramatic and is now a listed building. Its barrel vaults rise to a great height above the parking area, dwarfing men and even buses beneath. Ironically this form of construction was only chosen for speed of building, because there was a severe shortage of steel girders throughout the UK, and use of concrete promised an earlier start. That was not to be, perhaps because concrete beams also need steel reinforcement, and for that and other reasons work could not even begin when planned on this much-needed garage for the tram conversion scheme.

By the time North Street (Romford), Stockwell and other garages were underway, LT had refined its garage designs, one noticeable difference being in pit layout. What were called 'swimming pool'-type pits had a wider open area (protected by a removable grating) on one side to make working on underfloor-engined vehicles easier.

Bus design has changed greatly since the 1950s, and the rear-engined vehicle has become universal. Floor-mounted jacks have become common in commercial garages and offer all-round access to the whole of the underside of a bus. But they are never likely to become common in London garages since there is insufficient height available for lifting double-deckers. However, a neat division of work can be found at Westbourne Park, where the existing pits (built for fewer than half the number of buses now allocated) are used for the low-floor rear-engined double-deckers and for RMLs, while another section of the garage houses the lifting jacks that are used for servicing and maintenance on the rear-engined Dennis Darts.

Something else that has changed over the years is the range of skills found in London garages. Particularly in the years before Chiswick Works began centralised overhauls of buses in 1921, there was a wide range of crafts-men employed at every LGOC garage. Partly this was brought about by the Metropolitan Police requirement for an annual overhaul for every vehicle. The blacksmith formed an important (and some would say unfortunate) part of the maintenance and repair team, but in those days when metallurgy was not widely understood the LGOC discovered that enthusiasm for heating parts in a fire to bend them, or to straighten them, was causing all kinds of premature component failures. That apart, early bus garages were relatively self-contained affairs, with a staff fully able to repair, maintain and overhaul the run-ning gear of a vehicle, using (mainly) hand tools. Bodies were often overhauled elsewhere, with the chassis then driven back to its home garage to be worked on. As a first step towards inevitable centralisation of overhauls at Chiswick, there was an interim stage when four garages gained staff from other garages so that overhauls could be undertaken at just these locations. Then, when Chiswick Works was more-or-less completed, such work ceased at the four garages and the staff were moved to Chiswick.

Even before World War 1, some surprising tasks had been undertaken at garages. For example, in 1911, when a few hundred of the legendary B type had been built, it was decided to transfer a considerable number of bodies taken from older Straker-Squires, Milnes-Daimlers and Wolseleys on to the new B-type chassis. More than 70 such body swaps were carried out at

Above:
The requirement for an annual FFD (freedom from defect) certificate eliminated the need for heavy overhauls of buses at infrequent intervals and hence the requirement for large engineering workshops such as Aldenham or Chiswick. Here an RM receives heavy attention at the Willesden base of BEL (Bus Engineering Ltd). But the move from Chiswick to a smaller site and diversification into work on lorries and vans was insufficient to make BEL profitable. *Stephen Morris*

Battersea, Cricklewood, Norwood and Old Kent Road garages. After the end of the war, when police approval was being sought for use of some heavier B-type chassis using spare parts made in the US, Willesden garage even assembled four such chassis, the first being a bus and the others lorries.

During and immediately after World War 2 a number of garages undertook body overhauls, but such work was soon centred mainly on the Chiswick overhaul works and with a number of outside contractors. In due course Aldenham Works became the overhaul centre for all types, with Chiswick reconditioning mechanical components. That marked the ultimate in de-skilling the garages: for example, after minor accident repairs to panel damage, the panels that had been replaced had to be sent to Aldenham for a decision on how much of the bent panel could be reused. The local man was not trusted to make his own decision.

The routine docking of vehicles has always been a part of garage procedure, but that was another part of the workload that was to reduce in the 1950s. So reliable had the RT family become that what was known as the secondary nine-week and major 27-week docking of vehicles was dropped and replaced by larger three-weekly

inspections. Most parts were no longer replaced on a mileage or time basis but when worn out (or broken?), and all work was to be done at home garages and mainly between peak hours. At the same time, spare buses were apparently cut to a margin of just 5%. This was a big change from previous practice and differed greatly from the previous system whereby garages were grouped together with major work being done by just one garage in the group. For example, the dock unit at Norbiton (which was separate from the main garage) was designed and built to handle not only Norbiton's buses but also those from Kingston (K), Twickenham and Mortlake. Similarly, an imposing new docking unit on what had been a parking area at one end of Camberwell garage (Q), was designed to handle also buses from neighbouring Walworth (WL) — a total of some 350 buses. Today the Camberwell unit is an essential part of operations at that garage, while the one at Norbiton, like its running shed on the other side of the road, has long since gone.

But while the 1950s saw a run-down in the amount of work done at garages, European legislation some 30 years later was to transfer work back to garages and contribute to the closure of Aldenham and Chiswick.

Right:
Many minor tasks are undertaken at garages. Here two staff at Dalston garage are updating destination blinds. *Capital Transport*

Below:
Checking the water level is a routine task before a driver takes out a bus. Here the radiator of an Olympian is topped up at Croydon garage. Exhaust fumes from cold engines have been reduced since low-sulphur fuel has been used. *Author*

Previously, buses had, when new or usually after overhaul, gained a seven-year Certificate of Fitness; EC-derived laws decreed an annual test, called FFD — Freedom from Defects. That did away with the point of light or heavy overhauls (and hence Aldenham's work in particular) and substituted the need for a much more frequent outside check on the condition of vehicles — a check which, incidentally, insists on bus windows being undamaged by graffiti or scratching. By the time FFD came along, London's garages had already been grouped in a number of larger units, and each unit then chose one garage to handle its FFD work. A similar system still prevails today.

It seems unlikely that we shall ever again see splendid new bus garages being built, but, in a 31-point plan announced in June 2001, Transport for London did promise to seek out new sites for use as bus garages, which would be available for leasing by potential operators. There could also be some reduction in the number of former LT garages used by the present mainstream operators, since after 2004 the 'claw-back' provisions on property, introduced when London Buses' subsidiaries were privatised, expire. Then companies can, if they wish, sell them, though of course they will have to find accommodation elsewhere for the buses.

Garages closed before privatisation

The replacement of the remaining trams and later of the trolleybuses led to the closure of a number of garages and depots. New buildings replaced some of the oldest or most cramped. The decline in passenger numbers, particularly after the disastrous bus strike of 1958, led to further closures, and subsequently a programme to build new garages saw some others replaced.

But the largest number of closures came in the run-up to privatisation, when some 20 were regarded as surplus to requirements; they were not wanted by the embryo companies. The pressures of high overhead costs, rates and other outgoings were seen too great if a garage was, say, only half full.

LT promptly sold off just four of the 20 — Muswell Hill (MH), Norbiton (NB), Walthamstow (WW) and West Ham (WH) — for a total of £5.24 million in 1994, citing the high development value of their sites. One other garage, Twickenham, that had closed earlier was also sold at the same time.

Several garages have disappeared completely, with even the road or roads they stood in having totally vanished. Others still stand, perhaps empty or as part of some supermarket or other development.

One or two of the more recently-built garages feature in this list, perhaps because their well-appointed features made them more expensive to run, or perhaps because they were just too near another garage.

ABBEY WOOD (AW)
Abbey Wood Road

Abbey Wood garage began life as a tram depot, opened in April 1910 after the LCC had extended its electric trams from Plumstead to Abbey Wood. Tramcars for the new depot were brought by rail to the nearby Abbey Wood station and then delivered on a horse-drawn wagon to the depot. Extension of the electric services towards Central London brought a need for more cars, and Abbey Wood was extended to take 86 cars instead of its original 25.

It was one of London's last depots to operate trams, finishing on 5 July 1952 — the final day of tramway operations. A new office and canteen block was built and the tram shed reconstructed to take buses, though all was not ready for 6 July. It provided some 20 RTLs for

Left:
A solitary tram stands partly in and partly outside Abbey Wood on the last day of tram operation. From the following day only some of the replacing buses could be housed in the building. *Author*

new route 177, plus three on Sundays for route 182. But there was not enough room for all its allocation, so RTLs for route 186 were based at Saunder's Yard in Southland Road, near Plumstead garage, until early September, the staff and buses being officially allocated to Plumstead for this period. Many of the RTLs when first allocated had a run-down appearance, since they had been used for driver training for the previous stages of the tram conversion programme. For a while too, the traverser that had moved trams about the depot was used to move buses, until the traverser pit could be filled in.

The RTLs were replaced by RTs in 1955, and RMs began to replace the RTs from 1968. DMSs appeared in 1972 and the last RTs had gone by mid-1977. MDs arrived in 1981, but some RMs survived until closure in October 1981. Not long before closure to trams, some 56 had been required at peak times. Scheduled requirements for the replacing buses (including those based at Saunder's Yard) were under 40 and this kind of total was typical for most of the remaining 29 years. But by the end they were spread over more routes; from February 1981 onwards, MDs from New Cross were transferred here and worked all five routes allocated. Like Plumstead (AM), the garage was replaced by the new Plumstead (PD) garage. The Thamesmead area north of Abbey Wood was growing, and the Abbey Wood garage could not conveniently be enlarged.

ATHOL STREET, POPLAR (C)

Athol Street (a road parallel to the East India Dock Road and approached via Aberfeldy Street)

No doubt because of its long connection with the bus routes through the Blackwall Tunnel (and to a lesser extent, the Rotherhithe Tunnel), Athol Street is one of the better-remembered bus garages, though it closed over 40 years ago. The garage was near the northern entrance to the Blackwall Tunnel, and its origins dated back to 1879 when the LGOC acquired a lease (for £131 5s a year) on a site adjacent to the shed and stables already occupied by the North Metropolitan Tramways Company. It opened in 1879, became a bus garage in 1907 and closed in May 1961. Its proximity to the docks meant that it became LT's most frequently bombed property in World War 2, when much of the area surrounding it was flattened.

B-type single-deckers began a service through the Blackwall Tunnel in 1912, but the route became of much greater interest from 1927 when special NS buses were introduced. Unusually for the time, most had enclosed staircases, but the heavily-domed roofs restricted seating on the upper deck: it was fitted down the middle in a kind of knife-board arrangement, with sunken gangways on each side. Replacement came in 1937, with a special batch of 40 STLs, which (unlike the NSs) were of

course, on pneumatic tyres, albeit tyres with reinforced sidewalls to withstand the continual rubbing against the kerb in the narrow roadway. In their earlier days, at least, the NSs would have had no windscreens, and it is said that crews were paid an extra 4d a day milk money to compensate for the smoke and fumes in the tunnel. Changes to the road surface in the Blackwall Tunnel enabled standard RTLs to replace the STLs in 1953, though the buses were still fitted with tyres with reinforced sidewalls.

One result of the bombing of the area, mentioned earlier, was damage to the internal railway run by the Port of London Authority, and the subsequent replacement of its passenger services by buses. Athol Street ran two STLs and subsequently RTLs on this service from Custom House station to Manor Way station.

The garage closed in May 1961 — later than intended, because its close proximity to East India Dock Road had enabled it to be used for meal reliefs; Poplar, which was to take over most of its work, was too far from the main road. Closure was therefore delayed until a new canteen, known as the Aberfeldy, could be opened on East India Dock Road.

At closure there were 52 RTLs on six routes, plus two of the small class of private-hire RFW coaches; all moved to Poplar except for the PLA service, which went to Bow, which had taken over the Clay Hall allocation on the service when the latter closed in 1959. Today the whole area has changed. The road has totally vanished, and trees and flats occupy the site and the surrounding area.

BATTERSEA (B)
Hester Road, Battersea

Battersea garage was opened by the London Road Car Company on the north side of Hester Road in July 1906. More space was needed quite soon, and in 1914 the LGOC built an annexe on the south side of the road. Internal reconstruction was undertaken in the early 1960s, and further modernisation in 1970/1 also saw the building of a canteen and recreation room in an annexe opposite the main garage.

One of the earlier operations from the garage had been route 19, which later reappeared in a yard at Hester Road under the auspices of Kentish Bus. Fleet modernisation after World War 2 saw RTLs and RTWs allocated. RTLs survived until 1967, when they were replaced by RTs, but the RTWs had gone two years previously. Clearance problems delayed the allocation of RMs until the floor level was lowered for them to arrive for route 22 in 1967. DMSs came in 1972, being replaced by Ms in 1983. However, the garage closed in November 1985, with its allocations transferred to Victoria and Wandsworth garages.

Battersea was later reopened to house London Buses' coaches and Round London Sightseeing Tour vehicles — an operation which subsequently became London Coaches. That operator also ran the C3 Chelsea Harbour Hoppa from there, but the whole fleet transferred to Wandsworth garage in April 1988. Go-karts can now be found running in what was the main garage at Battersea.

Above:
Carshalton was probably hardly ever filled to capacity in its existences as tram or trolleybus depot or bus garage. However, most of the fleet was out in service when this picture was taken. *Author*

Below:
Carshalton is still recognisable as a former London Transport garage in 2001. The London General Olympian passing it is on the 154, a route once worked by Carshalton. *Author*

CARSHALTON (CN)
(Sutton until July 1950)
Westmead Road, adjoining junction with Harold Road

This was first a tram depot, then a trolleybus depot and finally (and briefly) a bus garage. With an allocation of just 24 RTs it was London's smallest 'red' garage, so closure was perhaps not surprising. But the depot still survives in industrial use, and the office block by the entrance makes its previous use by LT obvious.

The depot was opened by the South Metropolitan Electric Tramways in 1906 for its new Sutton–Croydon tram route and had space for 60 tramcars as well as substantial workshop facilities. However, SMET cars were later sent to the MET works at Hendon for overhaul, and the workshops were therefore dismantled.

Substantial rebuilding was undertaken for the conversion to trolleybus operation, this being one of the first depots to be altered. An ornamental gateway was taken down to widen access, and a traverser and a turntable were installed inside the building. A new office block was built to one side as well as canteen and recreational facilities. Trolleybuses began running in December 1935, when the Sutton–Croydon route was converted. The following February the route was extended to Crystal Palace, and was the only route operated by the depot. The 654 was one of the more interesting trolleybus routes as it traversed the steep Anerley Hill on the approaches to Crystal Palace, and the vehicles were of the short 'B1' class with anti-run-back brakes.

Conversion for motor-bus use began in spring 1958 and included provision of fuelling islands and vacuum-cleaning equipment plus an Essex bus washer. Two 5,000gal fuel tanks were mounted on one side of the forecourt, while the traverser was removed and its pit filled in. Bus operation of the two routes that replaced the 654 — the 154 and 157 — began in March 1959 with RTs. Although it had been a one-trolleybus-route garage, it had also provided some workings on trolleybus route 630 from Mitcham to Croydon on Christmas Days only. That route was still trolleybus-operated at Christmas 1959, but the garage provided RTs for this. 'Lazy' blinds (ie blinds showing both destinations so that they do not have to be changed) had been provided for this complete with the route number 630, but for some reason this number was painted out before the day. The garage closed in January 1964, with route 154 moving to nearby Sutton garage and route 157 to Merton garage.

CHALK FARM (CF)
Harmood Street, off Chalk Farm Road, Camden Town

Following the compulsory acquisition of its Albany Street garage (originally used by Vanguard) by the War Department in March 1916, the LGOC transferred its buses to its new garage in Harmood Street, Chalk Farm. The new garage was opposite the premises of well-known bus bodybuilder Dodson, which were later occupied by William Dangerfield's Carlton/Overground buses and the LGOC, which garaged some of its private-hire vehicles there. In 1933 the LPTB closed the Camden Town garage it had acquired from the BAT and moved these vehicles to Chalk Farm garage.

By the outbreak of World War 2 the garage was operating STLs and Qs. From 1940 to 1941 it undertook body overhauls. In 1949 it began to be allocated SRTs — those expensively reconstructed STL chassis

Below:
A Fleetline for busy Central London route 24 stands in one of the doorways of Chalk Farm in 1975. It was the later loss of this route to Grey-Green that precipitated closure in 1993. *Gerald Mead*

with RT-type bodies. When these were being withdrawn in 1954 it became the only garage to be operating simultaneously RT, RTL, RTW and SRT types.

The first RMs arrived in 1963, and in 1965 some of the experimental batch of 50 Atlanteans (XAs) were allocated for route 24; some of the latter were then swapped for RMLs the following year as part of the comparison trials. Another trial, in 1976, like the previous one on route 24, was with a single bus, a Leyland B15 (Titan) prototype. Later, in 1988, it was the loss of route 24 to Grey-Green that ultimately led to closure; the garage had gone from a peak requirement of 100 buses in 1952 to fewer than 60. Quite late on in its life, in October 1986, its mixed fleet of Ms, RMs, and RMLs were all replaced by Ts. Closure in July 1993 saw its total allocation for five routes all transferred to Holloway (HT).

CLAPHAM (CA)
Near the corner of Clapham High Street
and Clapham Park Road

Probably no other garage has had as colourful a career as Clapham. It began as a tram depot for horse-drawn trams, was later used for electric trams and was then totally rebuilt as a bus garage. After less than eight years with buses it closed, subsequently becoming a vehicle store before reopening as the Museum of British Transport. After the museum (minus the London

exhibits) moved to York it became a store again before being bought back from British Railways in 1977 for £750,000 — for use again as a bus garage. It finally closed in February 1987, with the local authority planning to build housing on the site.

The site had been acquired in 1885 for a depot by the London Tramways Company, a concern the LCC took over in 1899. It provided some of the first trams for the LCC's first electric tramway between Westminster and Tooting in May 1903, and its rebuilding was completed in March 1905, giving it a capacity for 176 cars. Work to prepare the depot for buses began in mid-1949, when some trams were moved elsewhere to give the builders room to start work. The first stage of the tram-replacement scheme took place in October 1950, but Clapham was far from ready, with much of the depot virtually 'open air'. It was further complicated by the fact that, in any case, Clapham had to continue running some trams (alongside buses) until Stage 2 of the conversion scheme. Clapham received 37 RTLs plus a further 19 that could not be housed there and were therefore worked from Camberwell garage. The second stage of the conversion, in January 1951, saw Clapham receive another 85 RTLs plus the 19 from Camberwell, to make it one of the largest garages in the fleet with 141 buses, albeit in a depot still far from complete.

The early tram-replacement services had been worked out on a generous basis of more than one bus per tram (to allow for the lower seating capacity of a bus), but this

was really excessive — the more so when traffic began to decline from the mid-1950s. Maintenance of bus garages was proving costly, and as a result Clapham closed in November 1958. Routes 155 and 189 moved to Merton, the others to Stockwell.

In March 1961 the garage reopened in its new guise as a national transport museum, housing railway locomotives and rolling stock as well as various preserved London buses, including B340, K424, S742, NS1995, ST821, LT165, T219, Q55 and trolleybus No 1. But in a decision that was controversial at the time, the Government decided that the best place for the museum was York, and Clapham closed its doors in April 1973. LT declared that its London collection should be displayed in London and retrieved all its exhibits for subsequent display at Syon Park.

After LT had repurchased Clapham, renovation work was undertaken including what must have been expensive work to eliminate roof supports to give a clear manœuvring area — an extravagance, surely, in a garage to be used only as a temporary replacement for others.

First admissions to Clapham came in April 1981, when Norwood's buses and staff were transferred to allow Norwood's reconstruction. Norwood moved out, as it were, in October 1984, and Streatham moved in, to allow rebuilding there, a process that lasted until February 1987. Norwood's buses temporarily allocated to Clapham had been RMs and RMLs, while those from Streatham were Ms, though these were

partly replaced by Ls late in 1986. The garage was sold for redevelopment in mid-1987.

CLAY HALL (CL)
Old Ford Road

This garage stood on the site of what had once been a pleasure garden, but the buildings and location have subsequently been engulfed within the motorway approach to the Blackwall Tunnel. The site had been acquired in 1897 for use as a horse-bus depot, and it opened for motor buses in October 1910 when it was allocated the first 60 of the new B type to be built. All went on to route 8.

Wartime brought the closure of the garage in April 1917, when operations were transferred to Dalston, and Clay Hall did not reopen until July 1919, for the operation of lorry-buses. It closed again in August 1920 and was then used as a store. It reopened the same day as the rebuilt Upton Park — 7 October 1931; rebuilding had cost £40,000. It then had a scheduled requirement of 48 NS types with covered tops, most from Dalston. Then, in the first five months of 1933, Clay Hall received 49 of the first batch of 50 STLs built; all were petrol-engined 60-seaters for route 8 and its offshoots. It was still an STL garage at the outbreak of World War 2.

After the war and as a result of bomb damage, two former roads adjoining (Summer Street and Spring

Right:
The new office buildings added to Colindale depot in 1936 can be seen on the right in this 1961 picture. *John Gillham*

Below:
Many trams had been scrapped on vacant land at Colindale depot, and some 35 years later most of London's trolleybuses met their fate in the same way and at the same place at the hands of George Cohen & Sons Ltd. *Bill Godwin*

Above:
A newly repainted Routemaster stands nearest the camera in this line-up at Dalston garage just before closure in 1981. It had been working on route 9, while others carry blinds set for routes 253 and 47. *Capital Transport*

Street) were incorporated into the garage area. Clay Hall was still an STL garage after the war, and the 8 and 8A still important routes, taking some 41 STLs between them on Monday to Fridays, plus another 28 STLs from Willesden garage. Clay Hall was also putting out another 16 STLs on the 60, an allocation exceeded by a contribution of 26 buses from Cricklewood.

Later the 8/8A were to become RTW-worked routes, with an allocation of 38 in 1955, while RTLs made up the total requirement on five other routes to a maximum of 60 buses. But the garage suffered from being located in a backwater because of a number of low railway bridges in the immediate vicinity which made access to otherwise nearby routes complicated. As a result, when the trolleybus conversion programme got underway there was sufficient room at Bow, which was very near, but on the right side of a low railway bridge between them. Thus it was to Bow that most routes went, with 37 RTWs and five RTLs, but route 56 went to Athol Street, Poplar. Bow also gained a one-bus allocation on the PLA service. But a last claim to fame from Clay Hall was as the first garage to be allocated the first production RMs, albeit merely as trainers for the trolleybus conversion.

COLINDALE (CE)
(Hendon until July 1950)
Edgware Road, Hendon, between the junctions with The Greenway and Annesley Avenue

Arguably this was London's first trolleybus depot, in that in 1909 an experimental trolleybus installation complete with a trolleybus was demonstrated within the precincts of the premises. Hendon depot was built by the Metropolitan Electric Tramways in 1904 and

came into use with the opening of the company's Cricklewood–Edgware tramway in December that year. It had capacity for 32 trams. From 1908 it was used to overhaul trams and also to build new tramcars.

In 1912 a garage was erected on part of the site to house the motor buses of the Tramways (MET) Omnibus Company, operation of which started in 1913, but, following an agreement with the LGOC, the buses moved out in 1914 and the garage was sold to an aircraft manufacturer.

Trolleybuses reappeared in July 1936, following considerable reconstruction. The original car shed was retained, but the rear wall was removed to improve access and a third bay was added to the building. New offices were also provided.

When the Central Road Services organisation was set up, the depot was renamed Colindale, to avoid confusion with Hendon bus garage. By then it was running 33 trolleybuses on three routes. It closed in January 1962, staff moving to Cricklewood and Edgware garages. Part of the depot site had earlier been used for scrapping trams redundant under the prewar tram-to-trolleybus scheme, and after closure the site was used to scrap most of the trolleybuses.

DALSTON (D)
Shrubland Road and Ivydene Road, Dalston

From 1870 and perhaps earlier the 1st Royal Tower Hamlets Militia's barracks occupied the site later to become Dalston bus garage. Indeed, parts of the cavalry barracks survived in the garage, which opened for motor buses in July 1906 when the Motor Bus Company, a Vanguard subsidiary with the fleetname 'Pilot', began working an Upper Clapton–Loughborough Junction route with 10 Milnes-Daimlers. A newspaper report in December 1906 stated that the garage was to be reconstructed to house 180 motor buses, so it could be that the garage was enlarged before some MOCs and De Dion Boutons were added to bring the number of buses on the route to over 30. Vanguard then absorbed 'Pilot' in 1907 and shortened the route. Dalston was closed for a time, but reopened in January 1908, the year it began its long association with the well-known route 11; it was still working the 11s when it closed in 1981.

Yet the 11 terminus at Liverpool Street was some two miles away, buses working to and from the garage in service. Soon after the outbreak of World War 2, part of route 76 was reallocated from Tottenham to Dalston (the garage from which it first worked in 1912) in order to reduce workings that were remote from their garages, a feature that remained at Dalston. At the outbreak of war Dalston's allocation consisted of STLs and LT single-deckers.

The garage had a strong engineering tradition. In 1921 it had been one of four which took on overhaul of chassis and mechanical components before Chiswick Works became operational. From the 1950s onwards it ran a number of trials of single-deckers; the proximity of a number of low railway bridges in the area gave it two routes — 208 and 208A — which had some tight turns and corners and were heavily used. In the early postwar years they were worked with a mix of side-engined Q-type and LT single-deckers, and the replacement of the LTs removed the last three-axle buses from regular service with London Transport. RFs then had a long reign at the garage, and when route 236 (operated jointly with Leyton garage) went over to SMSs in 1971 it brought to an end the last single-deck crew operation in the Central Area. Earlier, in 1959, to cut down on uneconomic single-deck operation, route 208A had been converted to low-height RLH double-deckers, being renumbered 178 at the same time. The RLHs also went in April 1971, and were the last in the Central Area; their replacement was by MBSs working on new route S3, which did not, however, cover all of the old 178.

Unusual vehicles tried on the 208 were a Bristol/ ECW LS, the prototype AEC/Park Royal Regal IV (now preserved) and a Leyland/Saunders-Roe Tiger Cub, from November 1953. In 1973 six Metro-Scania single-deckers and six Leyland Nationals were tried on the S2; the Metro-Scanias (MSs) stayed nearly three years before being replaced by SMSs, but the Leyland Nationals (LSs) moved away earlier, to join a later and much larger batch at Hounslow. The MBSs went in 1976, but the SMSs survived until late 1979, with LSs reappearing and gradually taking over from 1978 and remaining until closure.

Postwar double-deckers were RTs, joined later by RTWs. In 1954 RTLs replaced the RTs, only to be replaced by RTs again in 1968. RMs ousted the RTWs in 1963, and also stayed till closure. The garage had had a peak requirement of 127 buses in the early postwar years, but this had dropped to 70 in 1976; at closure (when almost all work moved to Ash Grove) only one route passed near the garage out of the seven operated.

EDMONTON (EM)
Tramway Avenue, Edmonton

Tramway Avenue is still a turning off the Hertford Road today, though the depot it led to has been completely demolished. The thoroughfare was laid from the main road to reach the new depot built by the North London

Above:
At the end of Tramway Avenue was Edmonton depot, closed in 1986. The road still retains its original name today.
John Gillham

Suburban Tramways Company in 1880/1. Between 1885 and 1891 the depot housed steam tram locomotives and cars for the North London Tramway Company, one of the few examples of steam traction on London's tramways. Usage then reverted to horse trams, operated by the North Metropolitan Tramways Company.

The depot passed to Metropolitan Electric Tramways in 1902 and was reconstructed ready for the electric trams which came into operation in July 1905. Further extensions took place in 1907 and 1912. It was again modified, for trolleybus operations, with the trolleybuses coming into service in October 1938. It had an official capacity for 122 trolleybuses and, in 1950, was putting out a maximum of 116 at rush hours.

The last trolleybuses ran in July 1961, but it was a staged changeover starting in the April, when 73 RMs were allocated. At that date it also temporarily housed RMs for route 253 until Stamford Hill was ready to receive them. Part of the large garage was then closed off, and later was used to store tunnel segments for the new Victoria Line.

RMs remained until the closure of the garage in January 1986, when most services moved to Enfield after rebuilding work there. Later, DMSs and DMs were also allocated until being themselves replaced by Metrobuses.

ELMERS END (ED)
Elmers End Road, and Beck Lane, Elmers End

This was a 'show' garage when opened in March 1929, built by the LGOC to incorporate all the features it thought desirable in a bus garage. It was light and airy, with much use made of glazed tiles; it had plenty of space for buses running in to wait before being refuelled and cleaned and it had a water-sprinkler system to guard against fire. Internally, the roof was said to be high enough not to decapitate anyone standing upstairs on

an open-top bus! In its early days the garage received NSs, but by 1936 it had a mixed fleet of STs, STLs and NSs. All were then replaced by LTs, and at the outbreak of World War 2 the allocation comprised both single-deck and double-deck LTs.

The war brought tragedy, when in 1944 a V1 flying bomb hit the main entrance and exploded, with fire following. Seven staff were killed. No fewer than 31 buses were destroyed and a further 19 lost their bodywork. A number of the buses were from other garages, as Elmers End was one of those which carried out body overhauls. Despite the destruction, body overhauls resumed, and continued until 1946.

Rebuilding was carried out after the war and, when this was complete, a plaque was unveiled in memory of the staff killed; the Beck Lane entrance was named the Cunningham Gate in memory of the staff member who had died after giving warning of the approaching V1. The new garage was steel-framed with brick facings, and featured a parking area measuring 220ft by 135ft and a servicing area of 175ft by 40ft. There was a single-span roof, and some of the pits which survived from the old garage were altered to permit them to be covered over for extra parking space if required. Even before the new garage was completed it had a requirement for 91 buses — only two short of the theoretical capacity of the new building.

The first RTs arrived at the garage in 1948, gradually taking over all the work. But an unusual allocation in 1951 was of up to 10 STLs, which type the garage had not operated since 1936. They were to work serving Battersea Park special Festival of Britain services B and F. Otherwise RTs had a monopoly until 1973, apart from a three-year RM interlude on route 64 in the early 1960s. RMs reappeared in 1973 alongside DMSs, the two types ousting the RTs. SMSs were allocated from 1970 until 1977 when LSs took over. The garage closed in October 1986, and housing now occupies the site.

Above:
With traverser pit prominent, Finchley depot is seen in trolleybus days. The vehicles with their backs to it are over the maintenance pits. *Author*

Right:
The approach to the premises was surprisingly attractive, as is apparent from this summer 1990 view. The tanker was delivering fuel. *Kevin Lane*

FINCHLEY (FY)
Rosemont Avenue, Finchley and Woodberry Grove
(and backing on to Christchurch Avenue)

When the site for this depot was acquired by the Metropolitan Electric Tramways in 1904 it was more-or-less in the middle of a private estate, and a new road (Rosemont Avenue) had to be built to it. The depot opened in June 1905 with room for 60 tramcars and was extended in 1912 with a frontage to the Great North Road, but with no access from it. Considerable alterations were made in 1930 and 1931, with the shed being lengthened and a traverser installed to accommodate the new 'Feltham' tramcars, which were much longer than others. Yet more changes came a few years later to accommodate trolleybuses, which began operating in August 1936. Capacity was for 108, but in 1950 the depot was scheduled to operate 79 trolleybuses.

More conversion work saw 25 RMs and 15 RMLs (the first to be built) arrive in November 1961, and the last trolleybuses ran in January 1962. RTs were also allocated to the depot, and from the early 1970s first SMSs and then DMSs came and RMLs went. The RMLs came back in 1978 and RMs went before the end of 1980, but RMs returned from 1983 to 1985. Ms had arrived in 1980 but at the other end of the scale were FS (Ford Transit minibuses) from the Hampstead Dial-a-Bus service in 1974: the service later changed to two routes on a fixed timetable.

After the loss of route 13 in December 1993, London Northern found it had three garages where two were sufficient. Routes were shared between the other two — Holloway (HT) and Potters Bar — and the garage closed the same month, with the last bus moving out in early January 1994.

Above:
Three fuelling islands are prominent in this 1960 view of Forest Gate garage; all the buses are RTs. *John Gillham*

FOREST GATE (G)
Green Street, Upton Park, opposite Cromwell Road

The Great Eastern London Suburban Tramways & Omnibus Company occupied this site in 1898. It later became the Great Eastern London Motor Omnibus Company, which began operating from this garage a motor-bus route between Upton Park and West Kilburn in March 1906. In 1911 the LGOC acquired the company. By 1918 the garage was housing some 120 B-type buses plus a garage lorry built on the earlier X-type chassis.

Route 25B (later 25) was one of London's busiest routes and in 1950 the garage was allocated some 81 new RTs, all for this one route. It was spare space at the newly-converted West Ham garage (formerly a trolleybus depot) that led to Forest Gate's closure in April 1960, although it was still quite a large and busy garage. Some 68 RTs and their crews on route 25 all moved to West Ham. West Ham was in an engineering group with RTLs and there should have been an exchange, but the Forest Gate drivers were exceedingly unhappy with the idea, and eventually it was agreed they could take their RTs with them. The 66 moved to North Street, Romford, and only the 86 (and the Saturday 145) went to Upton Park, a garage that was not far away from Forest Gate.

Other interesting vehicles allocated to Forest Gate in slightly earlier years were some 20 or so SRTs for the 66, and during Festival of Britain year it had run five STLs a day on route C between the South Bank Exhibition and the Festival Gardens in Battersea Park.

HACKNEY (H)
Well Street, Hackney

The LGOC's Hackney garage came into use in June 1911 and was located not far from horse-bus stables previously used by the operator but since disused and

Below:
Overhead wiring for trolleybuses is still in use outside Hackney bus garage in this 1959 picture, at a time when the garage ran Leylands. The two exterior lamps above the centre doorway are identical to those outside Alperton garage. *John Gillham*

not sold until after 1911. It became quite an important garage, operating a number of Central London routes, and by 1921 had an allocation of 60 buses, all K type. By the outbreak of World War 2 its entire fleet was composed of STLs.

By the mid-1930s terraced housing and shops in front of the garage had been demolished to become an open parking area, but part was subsequently roofed over, increasing capacity from 60 to 100 buses by 1939. After World War 2 a new frontage was added.

As befitted a garage working a number of busy Central London routes, Hackney acquired a considerable allocation of RTWs for the 6/6A, 22 and 30 —

more than 80 all told — and these routes also had allocations from other garages; this was in 1952 when Hackney also had STLs for the 106. RMs and later RMLs arrived when the RTWs went and DMSs came and went for the 106 in the 1970s, but the route was one of those which went back to crew operation, with RMs. In 1968 the garage gained two new Red Arrow routes, worked by MBAs, and still had one Red Arrow route plus four ordinary routes when it closed in April 1981 on the opening of nearby Ash Grove. The garage was later used as a local council depot, but a new LidL supermarket was built on the site in the mid-1990s — with open-air parking for cars!

Above and right
Hammersmith depot's use changed in 1960 from housing trolleybuses to providing a home for the BEA fleet operated by LT. In addition to the well-known 4RF4s, the premises were also for a time host to LT's forward-entrance Routemaster, complete with its luggage trailer. *John Gillham* (1); *Author* (2)

HAMMERSMITH (HB)
Great Church Lane, Hammersmith

The Cloud family had been horse-bus proprietors before selling out to the LGOC in the 19th century. Subsequently the family sold land in Great Church Lane to the LCC for it to build an electric tram depot. This opened in May 1908 and was fairly soon extended. Trolleybus operation began in September 1937, the depot having been modernised for its new role. One of the trolleybus routes it operated was what became the longest trolleybus route, the 630, which replaced London's longest tram route, the 30 (Harrow Road–West Croydon). A small

number of crews and trams had been provided by Thornton Heath tram depot, so, in the short term, rather than provide a small number of trolleybuses to operate alongside trams at Thornton Heath, its relevant staff were temporarily on transfer to Hammersmith. The war stopped the tram-replacement programme, and some staff were still 'on transfer' to Hammersmith when its trolleybuses were replaced by buses in July 1960.

Not far away from Hammersmith was Shepherd's Bush bus garage, which had been expensively and extensively rebuilt in 1954, but had been under-utilised ever since, so the crews and replacement buses worked from there. Originally, Hammersmith had been planned

Above:
The former London United Hanwell depot is pictured shortly before trolleybus operation ceased. Just visible on the right is the front of a Routemaster, while in the centre of the picture is one of the postwar trolleybuses later sold to Spain.
John Gillham

to be the last depot to change over, but it was brought forward because construction of the Hammersmith flyover would have necessitated much overhead rewiring. Putting more buses into Shepherds Bush garage meant ousting the BEA coaches that had been moved there from Victoria a few years previously, so they in turn were moved into Hammersmith, on which BEA took a five-year lease. However, LT had to spend nearly £40,000 on making the depot suitable for diesel-powered vehicles. Some 61 of the unique 4RF4 coaches were allocated here and were later joined by LT's one and only forward-entrance Routemaster, RMF1254, modified to tow a trailer as a trial for the planned fleet of Routemasters with trailers. The BEA fleet moved on again in July 1966, to the former Chiswick Tram Depot, which later became Stamford Brook bus garage.

HANWELL (HL)
The Broadway, Hanwell

When London's first electric trams were introduced in 1901 the new Hanwell depot of the London United Tramways Company played a key role: the main route soon became Shepherd's Bush–Uxbridge, and in its last years Hanwell was home to some of the famous 'Feltham' tramcars. The large 10-track depot was extensively rebuilt in 1936 for the replacing trolleybuses, which began working in November that year as route 607.

Today's bus route 207 covers substantially the same ground, while a limited-stop version is appropriately numbered 607. But neither works from Hanwell, which closed in March 1993, with double-decker operations moving to Acton, Alperton and Uxbridge, while a new midibus depot was opened at Greenford.

In its trolleybus days the depot had run at capacity level with an official capacity of 108 and, for example, a scheduled requirement of 109 in 1950; more than 80 of those were for the 607. Buses took over in November 1960, with a scheduled requirement for 92 RMs. There were plans too for enlargement of the depot to enable it to take up to 150 buses. Hanwell had some RTs between 1963 and 1965, and in 1967 some RMLs arrived, these going on to oust the RMs by the end of the following year. That same year also saw the arrival of some MBSs to work new local flat-fare routes E1, E2 and E3, but these were replaced in 1975 by DMS and SMS types.

The SMSs gave way to LSs in 1978, and early in 1981 Ms replaced both DMSs and LSs; when the RMLs moved out in 1987 the allocation became entirely M. The total allocation had dropped to around 70 buses, but modernisation carried out in 1985 and 1986 enabled many routes and vehicles to be transferred from nearby Southall (HW) when it closed in August 1986. The number of buses at Hanwell rose to a peak requirement of 107 working on eight routes plus a night service, but the garage closed only a few years later, in March 1993, and was demolished in 1996.

HENDON (AE)

On the corner of Babington Road and The Burroughs

Hendon was the first LGOC garage to be provided with a mess room and recreational facilities, but similar facilities were soon provided at other garages as a matter of policy. At this time — the garage opened in March 1913 — a meal of meat and two vegetables and a sweet course cost 6½d plus ½d for a cup of tea (together less than 3p in today's money).

In its early days the garage housed Daimlers of the Gearless Motor Omnibus Company and the Tramways (MET) Omnibus Company. Later it was to become the first home of the first single-deck LT type (LT1001), and in 1933 it gained some of the first STLs, which were 60-seaters. A mixed fleet of STs, STLs and NSs gave way in 1937 to all 100 of the new STD type — modified Leyland TD4s with Leyland-built bodies, buses with their deep engine note that were to become one of London's best-known types. At Hendon they were always immaculately turned out. The last of these prewar STDs was withdrawn from here in June 1954, though earlier the garage had gained its first postwar buses, RTLs. During the early part of the war it had undertaken body overhauls.

In 1952 the garage had a scheduled requirement for a maximum of 93 buses, split between STDs and RTLs. The latter had been allocated in January that year after pressure from Hendon staff over the fact that they had

to run crash-gearbox STDs, on a route shared with Cricklewood, which was running RTs. The displaced STDs went to Enfield, to replace utility Gs. By 1966 the scheduled requirement had dropped to 58 but included RMs, which by now were working on route 13, though on Sundays they also appeared on routes 113, 240 and 260. Modernisation of the garage began in 1972 but did not finish until 1974. Following its completion, DMSs were allocated, these in turn being replaced by Ms from 1980. The last RTs had been displaced by the DMSs, but RMLs replaced the RMs in 1976. In October 1986 route 13, the most important and central route run by the garage, was converted to M, this becoming the only type at the garage. But it was not to last, and closure came in June 1987, with the work moving to Edgware, Harrow Weald and Holloway garages.

HOLLOWAY (J)

Holloway Road, Upper Holloway, opposite Wedmore Street

The origins of Holloway garage went back to horse-bus days, since the LGOC had a depot and stables there in the 1870s. Conversion of the premises to a bus garage was completed in 1911. By 1912, B types were being operated, including some in the colours of the Associated Omnibus Company on such routes as the 4 to Bermondsey and the 43 to Muswell Hill. Single-deckers included B types and later Ks, while in 1931 some of the first batch of single-deck LTs were allocated.

When the LGOC began buying up independent operators, the second to be acquired, in February 1926, was the Central Omnibus Company, with its Straker-Squires allocated to Holloway, but they were replaced by four K types repainted in Central livery. Later the same year, four of the seven buses of the Holloway-based Alberta Omnibus Company were also put into Holloway garage, while the following year yet another K type replaced the single Straker-Squire of the Victoria Road Car Company of Victoria. Later still, an exchange of duties between the London Public Omnibus and the LGOC saw a further K type running from Holloway garage as a replacement. Most of these independents were running on the 27/127 group of routes.

Some rebuilding work was carried out in 1930 and some internal reconstruction in the early 1960s. Just before the outbreak of World War 2 the types based at the garage were LT single-decker buses, LTC single-decker coaches and ST and STL double-deckers.

The garage was one of London's busiest, with a scheduled maximum peak requirement in May 1952 of 166 buses, all RTs. Some SRTs were run in 1950/1, RMs arrived in 1963 and RMLs in 1967. The latter two remained until September 1971, when the allocation was moved to the refurbished former tram, later trolleybus depot (HT) in Pemberton Gardens. In 1950 this had changed its name from Holloway to Highgate to avoid confusion with Holloway bus garage (J) but after the latter closed reverted to its original name. The garage subsequently became a bonded warehouse for HM Customs & Excise.

HORNCHURCH (RD)
Hornchurch Road, Romford

The LGOC opened this garage as Romford in July 1924, but LT renamed it Hornchurch in 1935; it is actually about halfway between the two. It began operations modestly enough, with 10 buses for route 26 (Stratford–Brentwood), and was run as an outstation to Barking, but by 1934 its fleet had risen to a scheduled requirement of 44 buses as the area it served grew quickly. In 1936 a considerable extension increased its capacity to 70, and the allocation was promptly increased to 54 buses. Soon a big route reorganisation increased the requirement to 67 scheduled buses.

Most of the additional space won by the mid-1930s extension was obtained by providing a large open parking area at the rear. It was provided with heating arrangements for vehicles in cold weather — an early experiment with an idea that was to be more widely tried away from London after World War 2. However, no official comments appear even to have been made

Below:
The bus-stop flag has already been removed from the post and replaced by a portable 'dolly' stop in this view of the entrance to Holloway garage taken a few months before closure in 1971. *Gerald Mead*

Above:
Hornchurch became the first garage to be totally one-person-operated. Here a Leyland National leaves on a dull summer's day in 1982. *John Gillham*

about the system at Hornchurch, and subsequently most garages extended or built by LT continued to provide mainly covered parking.

At the outbreak of war the garage had a mixed allocation of ST double-deckers and single-deck LTs, Ts and Cs. Early in 1940, fleet strength had fallen to 55 scheduled buses, but local factories for the increasing war effort soon pushed the figures higher, to 76 by October 1942 and to 85 by October 1945; by May 1953 the total allocation was 100. From October 1947 all the double-deckers were utility Gs, a matter which led to increasing opposition from the staff, not helped when they were told these reliable but sluggish vehicles were modern and only about five years old.

However, the early deterioration of the bodywork on many Utilities became a new factor in the argument, and ultimately type and condition rather than age became the criteria. Festival of Britain requirements for STLs being less than anticipated, there was a big release of these in July 1951 when no fewer than 62 replaced Gs on the busy 175, shared with Upton Park. Later in the year came yet more STLs, while in December RTLs came for the 175, in turn releasing STLs for other Hornchurch routes.

One move that LT would later bitterly regret had come in 1949. By then a mere handful of Cs remained at Hornchurch for the 238 and 252; in July they were replaced by crew-operated T types, and the one-man agreement with the union over Central Area operation was allowed to lapse. It took over five years' negotiations to revive such an agreement in the 1960s at Kingston garage. Another instance of larger buses taking over a route came at Hornchurch in 1955, when four RLHs were sourced from elsewhere to allow the 248 to be

double-decked; only one of these was red, the other three being green.

But the big change to Hornchurch had come in August 1953, when the new garage at North Street, Romford, opened, at last eliminating all those buses parked overnight in surrounding streets. Until then the garage had had to bear the brunt of the extra buses needed to serve the big new Harold Hill estate. Among buses to be transferred were some of the unloved SRT class, plus RTLs and STLs and TD single-deckers. The move permitted work to begin on modernising the garage, which was still responsible for heavy docking of buses at the new garage.

Unfortunately in later years the total allocation of buses dropped to quite low levels. After the 1958 bus strike the vehicle requirement soon fell from 53 buses to 48, and, although totals subsequently edged up a little, they were never much higher. The RLHs were ultimately replaced by SMS single-deckers, which in turn gave way to LSs in 1978. Before replacement the SMS fleet rose to quite a high level with about 30 allocated, and from November 1972 there were increasing numbers of one-man-operated DMSs; Hornchurch was the first Central Area garage to eliminate crew operation.

Back in December 1929 the garage had been the first to receive the new AEC Regal T-type single-deckers; coincidentally, in December 1978 it became the first to receive examples of the new T class — Leyland Titans. It took a particular pride in its Titans, overhauling T1 and treating it as its show bus, and keeping hold of the other low-numbered Ts, but the sad story of LT's Forest District saw all of Hornchurch's routes reallocated to Ensign or Frontrunner, resulting in closure of the garage in September 1988.

ILFORD (ID)
Ley Street, Ilford (on the corner of Perth Road)

The Ilford Urban District Council had built Ilford depot for the opening of its electric tramways in 1903. Another bay was added to the depot in 1909 and further extensions followed in 1921. Later the depot was reconstructed for use by trolleybuses, which replaced the former Ilford tram routes in February 1938.

The depot is best remembered for being the only home of 43 trolleybuses, intended for export to two South African cities, which were diverted by the Ministry of War Transport to LT. It took from late 1941 to June 1943 for them to be delivered, and they comprised 25 Leylands of two types (electrical equipment differed) ordered by Durban and 18 AECs ordered by Johannesburg. Before they were delivered the forward exit doors were panelled over and half of the generous supply of opening windows were fixed permanently shut. Special dispensation had to be obtained to run them, as they were 8ft wide (6in over the UK legal maximum) and were also heavy. All were allocated to Ilford, displacing standard trolleybuses to other hard-pressed depots and allowing the last nine of 18 trolleybuses hired from Bournemouth Corporation (and used at Ilford) to be released — not to their owner but to Newcastle-upon-Tyne Corporation Transport, which was also suffering a vehicle shortage.

Service levels had declined somewhat by the time the buses-for-trolleybuses programme came along, and when the last day came in August 1959 Ilford depot was running just 31 trolleybuses. All were scrapped, staff and work moving to Barking and also to Seven Kings garage to drive RTs; RMs were not ready in time for the first few trolleybus conversions.

ISLEWORTH (IH)
London Road, Hounslow

Named Hounslow until the mid-1950s renaming, Isleworth depot was on the main road through Hounslow but nearer to London than the bus garage, which was just off the town's High Street. Built for the opening of London United Tramways' Kew Bridge–Hounslow extension, it came into use in July 1901. It was extensively rebuilt in 1935 for trolleybuses, the work including installation of a combined traverser/turntable to facilitate manœuvring. From October 1935 to the last day of trolleybus operation in London the depot supplied up to 25 vehicles for route 657 (Hounslow–Shepherd's Bush). After closure most staff moved down the road to Hounslow, and the depot was used for a time by the Post Office.

LEA BRIDGE (LB)
Lea Bridge Road, Leyton, between Westerham Road and Dunton Road

Known as Leyton depot until 1950, this depot could trace its origins back to 1889, when it opened as a horse-car depot of the Leyton & Walthamstow Tramways Company. Leyton Urban District Council acquired the company and rebuilt the depot to house its electric trams, which began running in 1906; there was space for 65 cars, with the former stables adapted as store rooms, a mess room and a recreation room. From 1921 its services were run by the LCC through a joint body on which both parties were represented.

Trolleybuses began running from the depot in June 1939 and continued until April 1959, when the staff

Right:
Two of the postwar 'Q1' trolleybuses stand at one of the two doorways of the former Hounslow depot, by then renamed Isleworth.
John Gillham

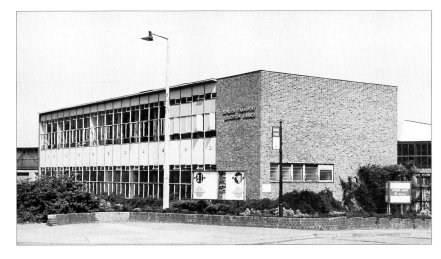

Left:
Exterior of the Loughton office block, set at an angle to and on higher ground than the main garage.
Gerald Mead

moved to Leyton and Clapton bus garages to run the replacement services. In its later days the depot was providing just a couple of dozen trolleybuses for two routes.

LOUGHTON (L)
Church Hill, Loughton

There have been two garages in Loughton, one on each side of the road, but ironically, while most of the older one still exists (as part of a supermarket), the newer one, opened in December 1953, has disappeared. The first was opened by the LGOC in 1923, cost £15,000 and could house about 40 buses. Its initial allocation was of open-top S types, and a traffic circular of the time reminded staff that 'all buses have to be in the garage by midnight'.

After World War 2, increasing traffic and new estates brought a need for a larger garage, especially as big new estates were planned for Debden and Hainault. But when built they were not nearly as large as originally planned, making the garage's capacity of 137 buses excessive. Some 60 new unused green RTs were stored there for several years, and at other times RMs for trolleybus replacement and surplus RTLs were also stored there. Part of the building was later let out.

A further blow came after LT came under the wing of the GLC. Both the garage and much of its route mileage were in Essex, and a lot of work went elsewhere despite the efforts of a very amenable staff. The final blow came when seven out of its eight routes were lost, leading to closure of the garage in May 1986; housing now occupies the site.

The second garage had been of standard postwar design, and with a separate set of pits for a major dock unit; major docks were undertaken for Leyton garage as well. The rear of the garage was of unusual appearance,

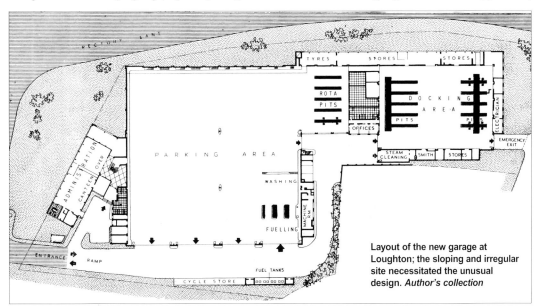

Layout of the new garage at Loughton; the sloping and irregular site necessitated the unusual design. *Author's collection*

as the site sloped away and much of the main floor was supported on exposed columns.

The old garage was London's first to run covered-top double-deckers, being allocated four such NSs for a trial to be observed by Scotland Yard. They formed one-third of the garage's allocation on route 100 (Epping Town–Elephant & Castle), a route selected for its varied territory which ranged from city streets to suburbia to country roads. The experiment began in September 1925 and was judged a success, with the LGOC being permitted to build a further 200 such buses. But the four NSs were taken away, moving to Palmers Green to work on route 29.

By the outbreak of World War 2 the whole allocation was LT type, all subsequently being open-stair versions. But late in 1946 it gained 25 of the new postwar STD type, ultimately becoming an all-STD garage (plus a few TD single-deckers). It never had an STL or an RM, and was the very last garage to gain an RT-family allocation — in 1955, when the STDs were sold off.

RFs replaced the TDs and later allocations were of MBs, SMSs, LSs and DMSs, with Ts arriving in 1982 to replace the DMSs but lasting just six months, after which the garage became all-LS.

MIDDLE ROW (NORTH KENSINGTON) (X)
Middle Row and Conlan Street

When Middle Row was opened in May 1910 the LGOC's motor buses ran no further out of Central London than Kensal Green and Wormwood Scrubs in this direction. Ironically, when the cramped Middle

Row garage closed in August 1981, its replacement was about half a mile nearer Central London.

In its earliest days Middle Row was home to all 60 of the LGOC's X type, the forerunner of the famous B, and the type which unashamedly cribbed anything that worked well on the LGOC's very mixed fleet of early motor buses. The garage had a long association with routes 7 and 15 — busy Central London routes still operated by Routemasters today, though not from Middle Row. The first RTs came in 1948, later displaced by RTLs which in due course were themselves replaced by RTs. The garage benefited from one of the later stages of the trolleybus conversion scheme from 1962, when it received RMs for improvements to existing bus route 18 and for new route 293. After the RTs were replaced in 1975, RMs became the sole type at the garage until its closure.

In 1952 the garage had had a peak requirement of 84 buses, all RTs; in 1976 the total was 63, all RMs.

MORTLAKE (M)
Avondale Road (off North Worple Way), Mortlake

This was the third garage to be opened by the LGOC for its new motor buses, in July 1906, but it originated as horse-bus stables built in 1901. Small artefacts from the original occupation were said to have remained until closure in 1983 and demolition four years later.

Soon after the opening, Col Frank Searle (who would later design the famous B type) was persuaded to become Garage Superintendent. That was in February 1907, and he received a salary of £350 a year. Some years later he described his experiences: 'Here I found the most colossal disorder that it has ever been my lot to

Left and above:
Despite its cramped layout, Middle Row garage survived for a long time; indeed, the building still stands today. By the date of these photos (1977) the whole allocation was of RMs. *(both) Capital Transport*

Below:
The north entrance to Mortlake garage in Avondale Road was the one most familiar to passengers and enthusiasts. Two passengers are waiting by the somewhat minimalist shelter to board the next No 9 bus out. *John Gillham*

witness. Out of 70 or 80 buses (all De Dion Boutons) only 25 per cent were in regular service. The old policy of robbing Peter to pay Paul had run rife, and buses were standing in rows minus gearboxes, front axles, back axles, etc. These had been taken out to make others run and unfortunately, no arrangements had been made either to replace or repair the defective parts.' Here was his glorious opportunity — 'a situation so bad that it must be improved by energy and a certain amount of horse sense'. The De Dion Boutons lasted at Mortlake until 1914, when they were replaced by a batch of 50 B types. Searle was a railway engineer by training and made quite an impression on LGOC management, for after less than three months 'of extremely hard work' he was moved to the much larger Cricklewood garage where there were worse problems.

In 1916 Mortlake came top on an order of merit chart showing the number of accidents per 10,000 miles run by each garage, and again had the lowest total the following year. In the 1930s it had an allocation of just two bonneted Leyland Cubs of the C class for route 207 (Barnes–Richmond Park Golf Club), a route that was indeed run for the benefit of golfers. It was abandoned in early September 1939 and never ran again. The rest of the allocation at that time was double-deck LTs.

The garage had a long association with important Central London route 9, which terminated at the garage, albeit for many years describing the place (as did bus maps) as 'Barnes'. RTs took over from the LTs in 1948 but were replaced by RTLs in 1955. RMs started to appear in 1962 and by mid-1963 had a monopoly until closure in June 1983; nothing larger could be accommodated. On closure route 9 moved to Stamford Brook, while the 33 passed to Fulwell.

Closure would have come as no surprise. Even in the late 1930s LT was looking at replacement, and then in the 1970s it was working out the logistics of closure and rebuilding of several South West London garages, including Mortlake, as detailed in Chapter 1. After the garage buildings were demolished the site was again used as a terminus for route 9 and later its successor at the outer end, the 209.

MUSWELL HILL (MH)
At the corner of Sydney Road and Hampden Road, Muswell Hill

The LGOC opened its garage in Muswell Hill in September 1925. It was then a growing residential area, and a major extension became necessary within four years to raise its accommodation to hold 30 more than the 60 that was the original capacity. Even that was not too generous, since in 1952 the maximum scheduled requirement was 99. Equipment included a sprinkler system, two washers and underground petrol storage tanks with a total capacity of 12,000 gallons. Just before World War 2 its allocation was all LTs, both double- and single-deck. During 1940 and 1941 body overhauls were carried out at the garage.

Below:
All the buses in this 1990 view of Muswell Hill are Titans. Note the sliding doors (centre left) to seal off the dock unit in cold weather. *Kevin Lane*

Above:
The Hampden Road entrance to Muswell Hill. *Kevin Lane*

From the opening, two single-deck routes (41 and 111) had been transferred to the garage from Holloway, and it became a predominantly single-decker garage in about a 60:40 split. Some of the earliest batch of single-deck LTs had been allocated in 1931, and these were to remain for many years. The garage received all 31 of the first series of TDs to provide the whole allocation for route 212 in 1946/7, causing similarly-bodied AEC T types delivered only months earlier to move to the 210, but that did not oust all the single-deck LTs.

An unusual allocation for some months in 1952 was of 24 former Green Line Q types for the 210 and 244 in response to continuing union complaints about the state of the elderly single-deck LTs (which by now were diesel-engined). There had also been passenger complaints regarding the need for umbrellas inside some of them when it rained! The first red RFs were delivered to Muswell Hill in September 1952. The TDs had gone by 1957 and the RFs by 1971, with MBSs coming in 1969 and SMSs two years later. SMSs survived until 1978 when LSs took over, but the latter went in 1986 when route 210 was reallocated to Holloway.

Postwar double-deckers were RTs from 1948 until 1971, RMs between 1963 and 1985 and RMLs from 1971. The garage was one of three to introduce the first crew-operated DMSs, in 1973, with one-person-operated DMSs appearing the following year, when DMs were also allocated. From June 1981 the one-person vehicles were replaced by Ms, and in the following year RMs displaced crew-operated DMs. Mid-1987 saw only Ms allocated. Closure came in July 1990, by which time just 58 buses — all Leyland Titans — were needed for three daytime and one night route.

NORBITON (NB)
Gordon Road, Norbiton
(by its junction with London Road)

Norbiton garage represented one of the sadder examples of how changes in demand and route tendering saw the end of a modern garage that had been desperately needed and had even been extended in recent times.

Nearby Kingston garage had been overstretched for years, and it was with great relief that Norbiton opened in May 1952. Even then, the new garage was less than ideal in that the site did not provide sufficient room for major docking work. That had to be carried out in a separate building on the other side of London Road, which dealt with buses from Kingston, Norbiton, Mortlake and Twickenham garages — about 275 buses all told. The dock unit was a former laundry, substantially altered so that it looked new, but incorporating the steelwork of the original building. Norbiton garage itself had a separate entrance and exit with a reinforced concrete canopy over each in a wavy formation.

Most of the routes and vehicles came from Kingston, the vehicles including 23 postwar Ts, 17 RTs (not all from Kingston) plus some of the oldest buses in the fleet — seven of the original Ts dating from 1929 for route 264, which crossed the weight-restricted Walton Bridge. A couple of years later the last of the postwar Ts were replaced by TDs, and in due course by RFs. In 1959 the first red RFs converted for one-man operation arrived, but did not see use as one-man buses until November 1964. BLs later replaced Norbiton's RFs, while SMs had appeared earlier, but when Kingston ran its (and LT's) last RFs in 1979, their work was moved to

Above:
The original Norbiton garage frontage incorporated an attractive undulating reinforced concrete canopy over the doorway. A postwar T, an RF, two RTs and an STL provide added interest in this 1952 picture.
Geoff Rixon

Left:
After rebuilding and enlarging in the 1980s Norbiton presented a totally different face to the world.
Stephen Morris

Norbiton for LS operation; the latter type was too long to be accommodated satisfactorily over the pits at Kingston, since the extra length would have impeded one of the entrances to the bus station. Norbiton's double-deck allocations over the years were rather more predictable, with RMs and DMSs, though the RMs came and went on a couple of occasions before ultimately being succeeded by DMSs, which in due course were replaced by Ms.

In 1981 a £4.6 million building project had begun to enlarge and modernise Norbiton and replace Kingston. A new maintenance building and office block was built on land adjacent to the former, the previous office building being demolished to allow more parking space and provide room for 116 buses. The corner of the new building was rounded to improve visibility at an awkward road junction. Because the site of the extension was previously occupied by a Victorian castellated building in Gothic style known as Snappers Castle, the new office building was also built in a style which suggested a castle. The extension was opened in January

1984, enabling Kingston garage (but not the attached bus station) to close — for the time being. Deregulation outside London encouraged the start of a new 306 (Kingston–Epsom) in competition with London Country (South West)'s established 406 in October 1986, but this was not successful. The following year saw the establishment of a low-cost unit named Kingston Bus, using DMSs resuscitated (none too successfully) from a variety of sources; this was a failure, with strikes and a High Court action over the poorer wages and longer hours to be worked. Another failure was a stranger commercial route, the K10, run with LSs between Kingston and Staines via a myriad of intermediate points; it was withdrawn in August 1990 after some two years' operation.

In September 1991 London United, the London Buses subsidiary now running services in the area, announced that Norbiton would close, following tender losses which left it with just two routes, but there was then an announcement of a reprieve to run the 57, but it closed the same month.

Above:
After closure by LT the former National Steam Car garage at Nunhead was occupied by Banfield's Coaches, whose proprietor had once been a bus driver at the garage. *John Gillham*

NUNHEAD (AH)
Nunhead Lane, Peckham Rye

Nunhead garage was built in 1911 for the National Steam Car Company, which ran its distinctive white steam-powered buses from there (and from a garage at Putney Bridge) until it ceased London operations in November 1919. The LGOC acquired the garage and reopened it in

April 1920. It was a building of a rather more attractive appearance than many of the time, with a two-storey frontage and a small domed clock tower in the centre.

By 1952 Nunhead's maximum peak hour requirement was for some 90 buses, comprising 31 RTs on the 12, 19 on the 37, 34 on the 63, and just six buses on local route 173. The last-mentioned was allocated five RTs, plus the one experimental postwar Guy, G436.

Above:
Later, Nunhead garage was used by Obsolete Fleet, which held an open day in 1981. A restored Milnes-Daimler of 1906 is prominent in this view, while also visible to the left is the front of RT1 (albeit now on a postwar chassis) and the rear of an open-top ex-Midland Red D9 double-decker. *Author*

Below:
Later still the garage was occupied by a distributor of beers and mineral waters. The tower survives on a new housing development. *John Gillham*

Despite the large allocation of buses, it closed two years later, in January 1954. In the same area were three other modern garages, two new — Rye Lane and Peckham — plus the extensively rebuilt New Cross. Nunhead's routes moved to Peckham and Rye Lane but in turn caused a related series of changes at New Cross, Stockwell and Walworth.

After closure it was used for a time for maintenance of the service or miscellaneous vehicle fleet, and in 1955 it also built the bodies to convert four STL chassis to towing vehicles. In June 1958 the garage was leased to London coach operator Charles W. Banfield, which was subsequently taken over by Ellerman Beeline Coaches of West Hartlepool, which used it as its London base.

Pioneering preservationist the late Prince Marshall later came to an agreement with Ellerman Beeline to use the garage for his Obsolete Fleet operation in 1979 and later also took over the workshop area too. Based there were the ex-Midland Red D9s converted to open-top and hired to LT for the Round London Sightseeing Tour, and the 1930 ex-Tilling open-stair ST922 used on the vintage bus service operated by Obsolete Fleet.

After Prince Marshall's death the premises were used for a time by a company selling beers and minerals. Part of the building collapsed in 1999, and that area has been redeveloped for housing, happily incorporating the original clock tower.

OLD KENT ROAD (P)
Bowles Road, adjoining the Surrey Canal

Old Kent Road garage was twice usurped by a larger set of premises at New Cross. It was originally the location of a horse-car depot of the London Tramways Company. The LCC took over the company, and converted the depot for use by electric trams — and then closed it when a larger new depot was completed nearby at New Cross. Vanguard bought the depot and converted it into a bus garage in 1907, and the following year the company became part of the enlarged LGOC. The bus garage closed in November 1958, with the former New Cross tram depot, now a bus garage, taking much of the work, while Peckham and Rye Lane also gained some. Some conduit tram track could still be seen in Bowles Road in the 1960s. The garage was later used by the Post Office, but Bowles Road has totally vanished, and the site is now part of the Cantum Retail Park, opened in 1992, with Halfords, B&Q and Comet stores occupying the area.

In its earliest days as a bus garage Old Kent Road operated one of the most varied fleets of motor buses in London. Soon after Col Frank Searle became Chief Engineer of the LGOC he had a big reshuffle of all the buses. 'Each type was given a garage by itself, and one big garage [Old Kent Road] was given for its sins all the oddments.' But things did improve, and in 1911 the garage remounted bodies from some 30 Straker-Squires on new B-type chassis for its own use. However, the garage ran nothing but open-top buses until 1934, when the roof was raised; the last Central Area NS open-toppers were withdrawn from here in April that year, and replaced at the garage by covered-top NSs.

Another noteworthy year was 1936, when in October the garage began operating the Inter-Station Leyland Cubs, with their raised rear section with luggage accommodation underneath. (The service had previously been operated by London coach operator P. Hearn.) The new buses were in a light blue and yellow livery and the route linked the main-line stations in London. In the latter part of the war and just after, traffic on it was so heavy that a number of ST-type double-deckers, with extra luggage racks downstairs, were used, being also painted blue and yellow. When the Cs were withdrawn in November 1950 London no longer had any petrol-engined buses scheduled for service. Ordinary RTs replaced the Cs, but the service was fading away.

The garage roof had to be raised again, in 1948, to allow RTs to enter. By the mid-1950s some 80 RTs were required, plus seven RFs for round-the-houses local route 202, which earlier had been operated by Qs. In the late 1930s, when the open-doorway front-entrance Qs were first put on the route, there was an alarming number of serious accidents to passengers jumping on or off while the bus was in motion and being caught by the nearside front wheel. A unique bus, allocated to the garage for a time, was the one and only postwar Guy double-decker, G436.

PECKHAM (PM)
Bull Yard and Hanover Park, Peckham

Thomas Tilling first leased premises at the Bull Yard Peckham in 1876, and early in the 20th century adapted them as a motor-bus garage. In March 1905 the company was granted a licence to construct four tanks with a total petrol capacity of 1,000 gallons, and this is said to be the first example of bulk storage for a bus company; petrol was usually stored in 2gal cans. From 1911 Bull Yard became the engineering headquarters where Tilling petrol-electric buses were assembled and maintained; bodies were also built there at times.

By 1940, following cuts in services, the Bull Yard was used to store a large number of vehicles, including numerous Tilling STs and 12 of the virtually new TF Private Hire fleet; one night that October, however, bombing and subsequent fire destroyed the premises and 48 of the vehicles parked there.

The first of the new garages planned by LT opened on the site in May 1951, its general design following new high standards. Buses entered from Hanover Park, and the three servicing lines for refuelling, vacuum cleaning and washing were grouped near the entrance and ahead of the parking area. The main pits, workshop area and stores were grouped together in an area with separate doors so that they could be heated effectively. As well as three Essex washers in the servicing lines, a new development was a roof-washing machine designed by LT. The maintenance facilities were designed to undertake major docks and other work for a total of 300 buses.

Above:
Interior of Peckham before it was fully completed, showing the unusual roof design. *Author's collection*

Below:
The exterior of Peckham gave little hint of its unusual roof construction. Routemasters dominate this 1990 picture.
Kevin Lane

Above:
The doors are closed and the original Plumstead garage is for sale in this 1981 picture.
After demolition a DIY superstore occupied the site. *John Gillham*

A major feature of the garage, though not visible from outside, was a reinforced concrete barrel-vault roof covering the parking area. It consisted of two rows of six barrel vaults, each 110ft long and 40ft wide, the dividing beam being supported by only two intermediate columns to give an almost unobstructed parking area of 52,000sq ft. More pits — for use in the overhaul rota as well as the day-to-day running shift — were in the parking area but could be covered over at night for extra parking space.

Operations began with 71 RTs from other garages plus a few new ones, because the opening of the garage allowed a big reshuffle of work affecting 10 other garages in North West as well as South London, though Peckham only took work directly from three other garages. Later the same month the garage also began running some STLs on one of the special Festival of Britain services and also housed those on another Festival service crewed by Catford garage, which had no room for the buses.

After the last London trams had run in July 1952 Peckham had a scheduled requirement for 170 buses, but many were temporary allocations until New Cross garage was ready to take all its vehicles. However, closure of Nunhead in January 1954 put more work into Peckham.

The first RMs arrived in 1963, these gradually forming a larger part of the fleet. RMLs appeared in 1971/2 and again from 1986. Local route 173 became the P3 and was one-person operated using some of the experimental XA Atlanteans; SMSs replaced these in 1973 and in turn were replaced by LSs in 1978. Some DMSs arrived in 1972, while March 1976 saw the first of 90 MDs (Metropolitans) allocated.

Early in 1980 it was decided to take doored buses off Central London routes, so RMs were reintroduced. When the new Plumstead garage opened, a decision to make it an all-MD shed saw 13 MDs transferred, necessitating the conversion of route 78 to LS operation, as insufficient RMs were available in the fleet.

In 1966 the scheduled allocation totalled just 99, but 10 years later had risen to 150, before dropping to 127 by 1987. The new BUSCO system of computerised bus control was introduced here in 1984 and fitted to the RMs on routes 36/36A/36B. However, closure and a move to a new low-cost base was announced in 1992, at a time when the allocation was 154, including 49 RMs and 35 RMLs. The garage was said to be expensive to run and there were worries about its ferro-concrete roof.

Peckham finally closed in January 1994. Route 36 moved to New Cross, along with its RMs, while the RMLs went to Camberwell for the 12 and 159. The rest of the work went to a new low-cost base in Copeland Road, Peckham. An extension to a Safeway supermarket and a new bus station now occupy the site.

PLUMSTEAD (AM)
At the junction of Kings Highway and Wickham Lane, Plumstead

Plumstead was still quite a rural area when the LGOC opened its garage there in October 1913. Indeed, just two years before, no General buses penetrated further southeastwards than Old Kent Road or Camberwell Green. Until the early 1950s the Sunday extension of routes 53A and 153 along

Kings Highway ran to a terminus shown as 'Bostall Woods', this later being changed to the more down-to-earth 'Plumstead Garage'.

The garage had not long been in use when it was requisitioned for war purposes, with its vehicles and staff having to be transferred to Old Kent Road garage. When it reopened in 1919 it was with an allocation of Traffic Emergency Buses.

From the 1930s Plumstead's allocation of petrol-engined six-wheel LT double-deckers with Wilson preselector gearboxes was unique, and some say they were the quietest and most civilised of all London buses. RTLs began to appear in 1949, and by 1952 there was a peak vehicle requirement for 92 of these, the greatest number — 28 — being on the 53A. In 1955, in one of the swaps that were such a feature of the times, the RTLs were exchanged for RTs. The first RMs had appeared by 1967, by which time the vehicle requirement had shrunk to under 70. Long single-deckers — MBs — appeared in 1969 for routes 122A and (later) 99, but after five years were replaced by DMSs. RMs were back from 1978 to 1980 on route 122, and in February 1980 MDs moved here, to be followed by more later in the year.

Closure came in October 1981, when Plumstead (along with Abbey Wood) was replaced by the new Plumstead (Thamesmead) garage situated on the site of part of Woolwich Arsenal. A superstore was subsequently built on the site of the old garage.

POPLAR (PR)
Leven Road

A tender price of £29,006 was accepted by the LCC for erecting car sheds at Poplar on a site acquired from the North Metropolitan Tramways, while adding paving, track and wiring brought the total cost up to £35,000. The new depot opened in December 1906, while its yard became the permanent-way depot for all the LCC's trams in North London. An extension of the depot to take trolleybuses saw the permanent-way yard built over, and the depot became the last of London's tram depots to be converted for trolleybuses, coming into use for the new form of traction in June 1940, operating four routes with some 70 vehicles.

But there was always spare space in the depot, and many newly overhauled STLs were stored there from

Below:
Preparations underway to convert Poplar tram depot for trolleybuses. The pits in the foreground are being filled for a new floor to be laid, with tram rail temporarily laid on top of the new concrete surface. *Author's collection*

Left:
In trolleybus days and for some time after, there was sufficient space to store vehicles. Pre- and postwar Ts and an STL are visible in this picture. The hand-powered gantry, just visible on the left, dates from tram days. *Author*

Above:
By the time this photograph was taken the garage was operating buses. The staff's cars occupy the spare space outside . . .

. . . and *(below)* yet more cars are parked inside, as well as some buses, in 1985. *Kevin Lane*

June 1950 onwards, ready for the extra services for the Festival of Britain the following year. Later it was trolleybuses destined for Spain that were stored and, later still, surplus RTLs awaiting sale.

November 1959 saw a complete changeover to motor-bus operation in the fourth stage of the trolleybus conversion scheme; previous stages had used the RT family, but this was the first to use the intended RMs, which also went to West Ham. Work on preparing the depot for its new role included provision of six 5,000gal above-ground fuel tanks feeding four fuelling islands, a Februat vertical bus washer and four modern tiled pits. A sprinkler system was installed, and an oil-fired boiler heated the offices, workshops and stores.

Poplar also became the only ex-trolleybus depot to operate RTWs. Following closure of the nearby Athol Street garage, it gained a one-bus allocation on the Port of London Authority dock service. This used an RTL, a type which swelled Poplar's fleet on Athol Street's closure. RTs later replaced them. In 1968 Blackwall Tunnel route 108 was converted to single-deck operation, using 50-seat MBs which were later replaced by ex-Red Arrow MBAs converted to a more normal layout. From January 1984 the garage operated new route D1, the Docklands Clipper, with specially liveried LSs; this was the first bus route to be started to improve communications in what was hoped would be a rapidly developing area. By this time, the double-deck fleet had become all-Titan, some being crew-operated. But closure came in November 1985, with the routes and buses widely spread: 15s to Upton Park, the 40 to Camberwell, 108 to Bow, 276 to West Ham, 277 to Clapton and D1 and S2 also to West Ham.

PUTNEY BRIDGE (F)
On the south side of Putney Bridge, near the junction with Putney Bridge Road

Early in 1913 the National Steam Car Company opened a garage next to the parish church and the bridge, at the end of Putney High Street. The company gave up its London operations in 1919, mainly because the cost of fuel for the steamers had rocketed. The garage was closed and sold to the LGOC, which rebuilt it and reopened it in January 1920. Soon some 70 B-type buses were allocated there. S types followed in 1922 and open-top NSs by 1924, covered-top versions following in a couple of years or so. Both STs and STLs were based there by 1936, though the last NS did not go until 1937. At the outbreak of World War 2 the whole allocation was STL, but that was soon to change.

The garage is best remembered for its 'prewar' RTs, having an allocation of some 60, the first delivered in May 1940. Together with Chelverton Road garage, it shared all 150 'prewar' RTs, though in their earliest days quantities were out of service while brake problems and other details were attended to. In the late 1940s the garage gained a few of the hired Tilling Group Bristol Ks, highbridge Eastern Counties examples being used on routes 93 and 96 — surely an enormous contrast with the air brakes and air-assisted preselector gearchange of an RT.

At the end of 1949, RTWs were allocated for route 85, and, later, postwar RTs were allocated too, only to be replaced in 1955 by RTLs. Internally, the garage was cramped and, with an allocation of some 100 buses, must have been difficult to work — a matter not made

Below:
An STL and a 'Bluebird' ST staff bus on trade plates occupy part of the rather spartan Putney Bridge garage.
Author's collection

This 1959 view of the exterior of the closed Putney Bridge garage shows that the frontage of the former steam-bus garage had been designed with a certain style. *John Gillham*

any easier by its direct exit on to a busy main road. However, its modest exterior design, with a semi-circular facade above the doorway, made it look quite attractive. But cut-backs after the 1958 bus strike brought about its closure in November that year. Most of its work moved to the other Putney garage in Chelverton Road, while the allocation for route 74 went to Riverside.

RIVERSIDE (R)
(Hammersmith until 1950)
Queen Caroline Street (originally Queen Street) and Great Church Lane, Hammersmith

A mansion named Bradmore House was sited on the land subsequently used for the LGOC's Hammersmith bus garage, and at the instigation (and with the assistance) of the LCC the bus company re-erected the old frontage as the facade to its new building, albeit facing a different way. By setting it higher than previously, the flanking windows on the ground floor were replaced by entrance (or exit) doorways for buses. Some of the ornamental balustrades and other details were retained, and, inside, some of the original decorative woodwork was repositioned in the new billiard room, to which the public was allowed free access on the first Monday morning in every month. The facade continued to survive when the bus garage was demolished, but it now sits somewhat uneasily among the modern buildings which closely surround it.

The garage opened in December 1913, and alongside was a covered way from Fulham Palace Road to provide interchange with the Underground railway station: route 33 stopped there, and the resulting interchange was claimed to be the first such between bus and tube.

Despite its auspicious start, the garage was probably never an easy one to work, with its internal pillars and awkward long roadway to the exit on to the increasingly busy Queen Caroline Street.

In 1923 the first production batch of NS buses was allocated for route 11. Later in the decade, when the LGOC began buying up the opposition, it replaced Florence's two normal-control open-top Dennises with two K types in Florence livery based here. By 1939 the allocation was entirely LT-type double-deck. Indeed, single-deckers only came on the scene much later, in 1970, when the first RFs arrived for route 290 when Twickenham garage closed; BLs subsequently replaced them. On the double-deck side, the early postwar period saw LTs and STs replaced by RTLs and RTWs. The RTLs lasted a particularly long time, from 1949 to 1965, while RMs replaced RTWs in 1966. Later, RMLs arrived, though when closure came in June 1983 there were still some 30 RMs allocated.

Closure was a relatively late decision, for in 1973 it was announced that the garage was to be improved. Later, as described in Chapter 1, there was the debate between the GLC and LT over the rebuilding of Chiswick tram depot to take Riverside (the garage had been renamed in the 1950s to avoid confusion with the nearby trolleybus depot) crews and buses while it was rebuilt. But on its closure it was merely announced that the lower service levels now provided could be accommodated at existing garages. After closure it continued in use for a time for buses terminating at Hammersmith Broadway.

Above:
The main frontage of Riverside (formerly Hammersmith) garage incorporated parts of a private house previously on another part of the site. *Kevin Lane collection*

Below:
Round the corner, another entrance in Talgarth Road had a totally different appearance. To the right was a walkway to the tube station. *John Gillham*

Top:
The exit on to Queen Caroline Street was not always easy ... *Author*

... and *(above)* parts of the interior were poorly planned for modern buses, as this 1983 picture shows. *John Gillham*

Right:
Closure came in June 1983. *Kevin Lane*

Riverside Bus Garage

This bus garage in Hammersmith will close after 24th June. The operation of its buses and routes will be transferred to other garages.

Bus 11 will run at the same frequencies as now but will terminate at Butterwick Bus Station instead of Brook Green Hotel in Hammersmith.

Bus 73 will continue to run daily between Hammersmith and Stoke Newington but will be revised to improve its reliability at both ends of the route. Extra buses will run between Tottenham Court Road and Hammersmith from midday until the evening peak hours on Mondays to Fridays. There will also be an earlier first bus from Stoke Newington to Hammersmith at 0506 on Mondays to Fridays. You'll still be able to buy your Bus Pass, Red Bus Rover or Travelcard at the following local places:

Peters Newsagents 93 Hammersmith Road
M M Patel 175 King Street
Hammersmith Underground Stations
(Red Bus Rovers and Travelcards only)

Above:
Substantial reconstruction and a modern appearance were not sufficient to save Seven Kings garage.
It was photographed soon after the work was completed. *John Gillham*

RYE LANE, PECKHAM (RL)
Bellenden Road, Peckham

Of all the garages built for tram-replacement buses, Rye Lane was the least fortunate, coming into use in January 1952 and closing in March 1969 — a victim of over-optimism, in the days when tramway substitution was planned,ᶜ and of subsequent falls in traffic levels. Research reveals that, in the reign of King John, Rye Lane was the site of Basing Manor. Much later, a horse-tram depot of the London Tramways Company had occupied the site, which subsequently became a tramway permanent-way depot. Site clearance brought to light long-forgotten drains and a well of pure spring water.

Whereas Stockwell garage had been built of re-inforced concrete because of a shortage of structural steel, Rye Lane was built with a steel frame because concrete was in short supply. The garage was really built to operate the bus services that replaced the Grove Park tram services and was allocated 87 RTs (not all new) to work five bus routes. One of these,

the 178, was a temporary allocation because Stockwell garage was not ready, and involved long journeys to and from Rye Lane to take up the running (or finish); it moved to Stockwell in April 1952. Subsequently the garage housed some of the buses for the 163, from July 1952 until New Cross garage was ready to receive them in late October.

At the time of the final tram conversion stage in July 1952 the garage had a maximum requirement for 108 buses, including some STLs for route 163 operated by staff from New Cross. But by July 1966 the total requirement was down to 87 — a mix of RTs and RMs — and a fair proportion of the work was on established bus routes rather than those that had replaced trams.

On closure the work went to Peckham and Camberwell. British Telecom subsequently used the garage, while the building later belonged to the Department of the Environment. It was finally demolished in June 2000 for redevelopment as a LidL supermarket — a fate shared with the former Hackney garage.

SEVEN KINGS (AP)

High Road, Seven Kings, east of Seven Kings railway station

Lack of co-operation between the various municipal tramway operators in East London hindered the introduction of through-running facilities, and made the area good motor-bus territory. The LGOC began a motor-bus service from Central London to Stratford, Ilford and on to Seven Kings in 1911, and followed this up by opening Seven Kings garage in May 1913. In the 1920s and 1930s the garage was also well sited for services in the growing residential areas of Becontree and Dagenham. In 1921 the allocation had been entirely of K-type buses, but by the outbreak of World War 2 it was all-LT.

The first RTs were allocated in 1948 but moved out in mid-1949 to be replaced by RTLs. Some RTWs joined a year later but after a couple of years were moved to Central London routes where their extra gangway width was considered of more use. RTLs remained until late 1958, when it became an RT shed again.

Under the third stage of the buses-for-trolleybuses scheme, the modest-sized Ilford trolleybus depot was closed and Seven Kings gained an allocation on new routes 169 and 193. Internal reconstruction of the garage took place in the early 1960s, and a substantial

refurbishment which drastically altered its appearance was completed in 1976.

Early in 1976 RMs began to appear, and by October 1977 the last RTs had gone. Routes not Routemaster-operated received DMSs from October 1976 onwards, but by July 1980 these were replaced by Titans; more Titans replaced the RMs by mid-1984. Striking new DA-class Optare Deltas were allocated from May 1992, being used on a number of routes, but the garage closed in March 1993 as the result of route losses under the tendering scheme.

SIDCUP (SP)

High Street, Foots Cray

S types were the initial stock at the new Sidcup garage when it opened in June 1924. The contract for its building cost £28,000, and it had room for 85 buses and was equipped with a 10,500gal petrol storage tank. It was always known as Sidcup garage, despite its situation in Foots Cray.

Just before the outbreak of World War 2 its allocation consisted of LT-type double-deckers and T-type single-deckers. It gained T types of the postwar style in 1948 and in the same year became the first garage to receive RTLs, these lasting until 1955 when RTs replaced

Below:
Sidcup garage's showbus, RM8 (the first production RM completed), in its pseudo-London General livery, is one of three buses occupying a quiet corner of the garage in 1983. Metrobus M805 (centre) was one of six allocated from new to Sidcup for comparative trials with Titans. *Geoff Rixon*

them. There were also a few SRTs for a short time in 1951. RFs replaced the postwar Ts in 1953 but were themselves displaced when route 241 was double-decked in late 1958.

Ten years later, MBs arrived for route 21A, but subsequent difficulties in getting them into the pit area for maintenance led to their replacement by the shorter SMSs, though these lasted only until the end of 1976. RMs appeared in 1975, followed by DMSs in the last months of 1976, and all the RTs had gone by mid-1977.

There was an experiment in July 1982 when six Ms and six Ts were run alongside each other on route 51 for comparison trials. Later the same year, large numbers of Ts were allocated, ousting the DMSs. The last RMs went in January 1986 and the last Ms in June that year, following the arrival of a small batch of Ls (Leyland Olympians) in April. From February that year the allocation was entirely one-person operated.

The garage had been modernised in 1972, when the open parking area at the rear was enlarged. Indeed,

Above:
An Uxbridge-bound trolleybus on the busy 607 passes Southall (previously Hanwell) bus garage. Note the turning loop across the dual carriageway for the trolleybuses. *John Gillham*

Below:
The bus garage is host to a new Metrobus, three AEC Swifts and a Daimler Fleetline in this 1979 picture. *Geoff Rixon*

there had at one time been talk of doubling the size of the garage, but over the years the vehicle requirement slowly but steadily declined: from a maximum of 111 buses at peak times in 1952, to 90 in 1966, and 77 in 1976, while the 1987 total was just 66. Closure came in January 1988, when Bexleyheath garage reopened; by that time, most of the routes that remained in Selkent District were more conveniently operated from there rather than from Sidcup.

SOUTHALL (HW)
(Hanwell until 1950)
Uxbridge Road, Hanwell

Opened in March 1925, the garage at Hanwell replaced a small one at Acton which could not be extended; today a new police station occupies that site. After just a few years, it was necessary to extend the garage, the work being completed in 1931. An allocation within another one ran from February 1926 for about two years when green K-type buses worked the routes from the Cambrian Coaching & Goods Transport Company; these ran with the code CA and not as HW buses. The garage was the first to run the ST type, being allocated the first 100 of them, of which some 72 were needed for its share of just one route.

Soon the garage was to become the chosen home for experimental buses, such as early diesel-engined LTs, including those with Gardner engines as well as the later and more common AEC-engined versions. Proximity to the AEC works was no doubt the reason for the choice of garage. Later the garage received a large batch of what are usually considered to be the first standard STLs. Just before the outbreak of World War 2 the vehicle allocation consisted of LTs and STLs plus single-deck Ts.

Because of its experience with Gardner engines (albeit six-cylinder versions), the garage received the first utility B-class Bristols in 1942, as well as later examples with AEC engines in 1945. It also received some of the early G-class utility Guys, but many of these were ousted by the later batch of Bs, though the last Gs did not leave until October 1949.

Some of the postwar STDs worked at Hanwell for a time, and single-deck TDs lasted until 1952 when Ts replaced them; RFs did not arrive until 1958. RTLs and RTWs were allocated from 1949, with RTs replacing them from 1951; the last RT did not depart until 1978. RMLs and MBs came in the late 1960s but the RMLs went in 1971 when some SMSs arrived, followed by DMSs in 1973. In 1978 RMs and SMs arrived, with Ms from 1979, the latter subsequently ousting the SMs and SMSs. After RMs departed in September 1982, the Ms reigned supreme until closure.

Vehicle numbers had remained quite high, from a maximum requirement of 112 buses in 1952 to 90 in November 1976. Part of the garage and a number of buses were damaged by fire on Christmas Day 1985. Closure came in August 1986, with work reallocated to former trolleybus garage Hanwell (HL) and to Alperton.

STONEBRIDGE (SE)
Brentfield, Stonebridge Park

Stonebridge was still semi-rural when a large area of land was bought for a new depot for the Metropolitan Electric Tramways to service its Wembley–Sudbury route. It opened in October 1906, and, six years later, more land was bought from the London & North Western Railway, whose tracks flanked the depot, to

Below:
Severe weather marred the last day of trolleybus operation at Stonebridge on 2 January 1962. Here RTs, Routemasters and a solitary trolleybus stand on the snowy forecourt. *John Gillham*

Above:
Two RTLs intrude on a long line of Routemasters inside Stonebridge garage. *Kevin Lane*

Left:
Part of the area outside Stonebridge garage was used for demonstrations on righting an overturned bus, using a 'prewar' RT. Here the bus is towed back into the garage in somewhat unorthodox fashion, attached to the front of an RTL which is reversing. *Author*

allow an extension. In 1920 some land was lost for building the North Circular Road.

Considerable lengthening was carried out during reconstruction for trolleybuses, and the depot was converted to a double-ended building to simplify vehicle circulation. It had a capacity for 86 trolleybuses when it commenced operations in July 1936. When buses replaced trolleybuses in January 1962 it was allocated 63 RMs and nine RTLs. RTs were later to replace the RTLs, in turn being replaced by SMSs, which were later displaced by DMSs. RMs were later replaced by RMLs on trunk route 18, but in 1979 were replaced by crew-operated DMs, with crew-operated Ms displacing them the following year. At closure in August 1981 the garage

was operating Ms, RMs and DMSs. The work and crews moved to the new Westbourne Park garage, but the crew Metrobuses went to Fulwell, displacing RMs to Brixton where they released DMs for Westbourne Park, all because it was decided not to introduce an isolated allocation of Ms into Abbey District.

Unusual allocations at Stonebridge were the remaining British Airways Routemasters, moved here from the former Chiswick tram depot in August 1978; the last ran in on 31 March 1979, when the service ended. Withdrawn buses were also stored at Stonebridge, and for many years a 'prewar' RT was based here for garage crews to learn how to right an overturned vehicle.

STREATHAM (AK)

Corner of Natal Road and Streatham High Road,
near Streatham railway station

June 1913 saw the opening of Streatham garage by the
LGOC, but operations began with blue B-type buses in
the livery of the Tramways (MET) Omnibus Company.
From 1917 these buses were repainted red, but
continued to carry the fleetname 'MET'. By the end of
July 1913 the garage had what was described as its full
complement of 99 buses and one lorry, the last-
mentioned being the garage service vehicle. Many of its

earlier operations inevitably competed with the trams of
the LCC and Croydon Corporation, since Streatham
High Road is a part of the main London–Brighton road,
and protests from the tramway operators caused at least
some buses to move to other routes.

The roof was raised in the early 1930s to allow
covered-top double-deckers to enter, and at the outbreak of World War 2 the garage operated just LT and
ST double-deckers.

From the 1950s to the 1970s the maximum scheduled requirement hovered between 70 and 80 buses.
Initially these were a mix of STLs and RTs, with the last

RT departing in 1975. The first RMs came in 1970, with SMSs arriving the following year for route 249 but being replaced by DMSs in 1976.

Some internal reconstruction of the garage took place in the early 1960s, but despite this it was announced in 1973 that the garage would be completely rebuilt. However, this did not commence until October 1984, when the routes, staff and buses moved temporarily to the reopened Clapham garage. Rebuilding cost £6½ million, and in its new form the garage had capacity for 90 buses — 23 more than previously.

When the garage reopened in February 1987 it had a peak requirement of exactly 90 buses. Routes 49 (18 buses on weekdays), 137 (13) and 159 (29) were all worked by RMs, while almost-new L-class Leyland Olympians worked the 50 (9 buses), 118 (13) and 249 (8) routes. But good times were not to last, and route tendering would soon lead to a number of route losses in South London. The upshot was closure in March 1992, with three 'big bus' and four midibus routes moving to Brixton, Norwood and Thornton Heath garages. All these garages (plus Croydon) were now in the South London company, which, following recent tendering losses, had too many garages for its remaining routes.

Nine years after closure, the garage remains intact; the forecourt or yard is still a turning-point for several routes, and buses still display 'Streatham Garage' as a destination.

TURNHAM GREEN (V)
Belmont Road and Essex Road, Turnham Green

There must have been parking problems in the relatively early days of Turnham Green garage, for late in 1911 it had an allocation of no fewer than 112 B types, many of which must have been parked in roads nearby. There had been horse-bus stables on the site from 1899, when some 34 horse buses were allocated. But a new garage was built and opened in May 1911; already some 62 new B-type buses had been built and stored elsewhere to await the opening. In the early days, and before Hounslow garage opened in 1913, some 'country' routes were worked from here, such as Hounslow–Windsor, later to be numbered 81. In contrast, a more 'in town' route was the 27 (Stoke Newington–Turnham Green), begun in July 1911 with B types.

Before the outbreak of World War 2 the garage operated only the ST type, but by the late 1940s it had become a base for elderly petrol-engined double-deckers of the STL type as well, with no fewer than 46 of these on the long 65 (Ealing–Leatherhead) on Saturdays and Sundays, with a few STs as well. RTs did not arrive until February 1948, for route 91, after the roof had been raised for them, and then in June the same year the first RTL (RTL501) was based here. The RTL marked what was to become a feature of allocations at

Below:
Interior of part of the Turnham Green garage, looking through the docking area (with some rather basic pits) to the main garage. *John Gillham*

Above:
Exterior of part of Turnham Green garage. Note the AEC Merlin facing out of the 'in' doorway. *John Gillham*

the garage: vehicles with experimental components — convenient, since Chiswick Works was not far away and could keep an eye on them. These included RTs with direct-selection gears, RM2 (after its brief sojourn as a green bus), early production RMs (just for a couple of months) and, from July 1977, the pre-Dennis Dominator testbed — a Daimler CVG6 fitted with a Voith gearbox. This bus, which had been new to Leeds City Transport, was painted red and worked on route 27.

The remainder of the allocations were fairly standard. In 1952 the garage was all-RT, with a maximum output of 81 buses, of which the 65 still needed some 50. By mid-1966 the total had slipped to 52 buses — a mix of RTs and RMs — and thereafter the fleet started to become more varied, with an allocation of the MBS type for the garage's share of the new Ealing-area flat-fare routes. The RTs went in 1971 in favour of DMS and SMS types, with the latter disappearing in 1973 but returning in 1975 to replace the MBSs, and then LSs replaced the SMSs in 1978. The DMSs lasted until the end of 1979, when Ms took over.

The garage closed in May 1980, when five day routes, one night route and 200 staff (including 160 drivers or conductors) were transferred to the refurbished Chiswick tram depot (now renamed Stamford Brook); the 47 buses moved comprised 16 RMs, nine LSs and 22 Ms. After the closure, Turnham Green continued to be used for minor modifications to buses, such as fitment of radio equipment, but nowadays housing occupies the site.

TWICKENHAM (AB)

Cambridge Road and Clevedon Road, Twickenham, near the River Thames and just south of Richmond Bridge

This garage was situated in quiet roads near the river at Twickenham and was once described as the garage 'under the evergreen oak' by *London Transport Magazine*. It had a chequered existence in its early days, and closure was mooted in 1939, yet this did not come about for another 31 years.

It was built on the site of a skating rink by the LGOC, and opened in March 1912. Early operations included B-type double-deckers on route 37 between Isleworth and Herne Hill. Not long before World War 1 ended it was commandeered by what became the Royal Air Force, which took over the building in January 1918. It reopened in June 1919, but ceased to be a bus garage in May 1921, being used instead to build bus bodies, which at the time were needed in larger quantities than Chiswick could produce. It reopened for bus operation in April 1924, and had its roof raised in the early 1930s for closed-top double-deckers. Nothing newer than NS types was operated until 1936, when the garage's first STLs arrived, but by the outbreak of war it was running only the latter type.

In 1949 the garage received SRTs for its two main routes — 90 and 90B — for which it needed more than 30 of the type. RTs ultimately replaced the SRTs and became the only type at the garage for some years, providing vehicles also for routes 27 and 27A, 71 and

Right:
A look into Twickenham garage from Cambridge Road; the date is 1970, and every bus is an RT. *John Gillham*

Below:
Routemasters — a type never operated there — predominate in this 1992 picture, when the garage was occupied by the Routemaster Heritage Trust. *Geoff Rixon*

111. In 1952 maximum vehicle requirement was 54 — a figure that slowly declined thereafter, although a reorganisation of the 90 group of routes in 1968 saw a few one-man-operated RFs allocated for the new 290 route.

Closure came two years later, in April 1970, with Fulwell taking over the 90 and 90B while the 290 moved to Riverside. Yet there was still a use for the garage, which was taken over by the London Underground's Engineers' Stores Department. The final flourish came when the garage was leased to the Routemaster Heritage Trust and became filled with buses once again, although, ironically, it was one of only half-a-dozen LT garages never to have run RMs. But the revival was to be short-lived — just two years and nine months. Despite being encouraged to bid for the garage, and having raised a considerable sum of money, the Trust (an offshoot of the Routemaster Owners' & Operators' Association) was outbid by developers. A very lavish brochure had been produced outlining the considerable attractions of the site, and smart flats now occupy the area, though a section of garage wall survives.

Above:
Two Red Arrows stand in the doorway of Victoria garage in this 1972 view. A visiting Standerwick Bristol VRL double-decker coach is just visible on the left, inside the garage. *Gerald Mead*

VICTORIA (GM)
Corner of Gillingham Street and Wilton Road, Victoria

This was London's most centrally located bus garage. The LGOC bought the land in 1930 for the considerable sum of £248,838, but building work did not start for many years. The garage finally opened for service in March 1940, with an allocation of 85 STLs for a maximum requirement of 79. It was renamed Victoria (from 'Gillingham Street') in June 1940. In October 1941 it gained some prewar RTs and, not that much later, 11 STDs (unfrozen Leyland Titan chassis with utility Park Royal bodies). It was the only garage to operate the latter type in passenger service, and they were withdrawn in March 1951 after drivers refused to operate them any longer. At various times it also operated some of the prewar STDs and some of the postwar batch, becoming the only garage to have run all three sub-types.

When the garage was first opened it took over some routes previously operated by garages remote from them, such as the 52 (Victoria–Mill Hill), previously operated by Camberwell, and the 10 (Victoria–Abridge), previously worked by Old Kent Road. But World War 2 killed one important aspect of the intended purpose of the garage. The site was chosen to allow rush-hour

Right:
The pit area at Victoria, with (on the right) the overhead track for a small crane to move any heavy component. Buses over the pits include the only rear-engined Routemaster (FRM1), placed here for the press to inspect the underside, as well as ordinary Routemasters and RTs. *Author*

Below:
Victoria often housed vehicles of other operators for fuelling and cleaning, particularly in the daytime.
Standing near the fuelling islands are an MCW Metroliner used on Armstrong Galley's London–Newcastle service and a Bova in National Express colours. *Author*

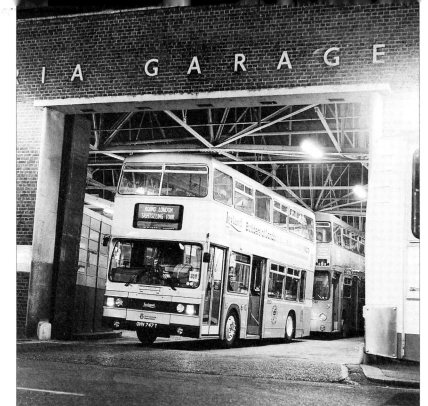

buses to be conveniently parked without incurring dead mileage in journeys to and from suburban garages. But it was also intended to be the new base for the Private Hire fleet, and was most unusual (for the UK) in being a two-storey garage. It had a basement area 230ft by 120ft, intended to house 70 coaches, and a ground-floor area of 350ft by 130ft. Separate ramps led to and from the basement, where the height was insufficient for double-deckers. However it did prove useful from May 1947 onwards when LT became the operator of the fleet of Commer Commandos bought by British European Airways for services to London's airports. These 18-seater coaches had a raised rear section, with luggage space beneath. As the size of airliners increased they became too small and were replaced by the more distinctive Park Royal-bodied AEC Regal IVs, on which the raised roofline ran the full length of the vehicle. They entered service, slowly, from May 1952, and then in October 1957 the whole fleet, by then totalling 65 vehicles, was moved to Shepherds Bush garage, allowing the basement to be let to the Post Office.

Most of the Private Hire fleet — or rather those that remained after bombing destroyed many stored at the Bull Yard, Peckham, in the early stages of the war — was distributed around several depots, but from June 1946 the Private Hire business and TF9 (the only surviving TF Private Hire coach, with its distinctive glass quarter panels in the roof) were allocated here, for use on two 'Seeing London' tours, one in the mornings the other in the afternoons, that ran from Victoria Coach Station.

Another postwar use for the lower level for a time

was for the daytime parking of the coaches used by Scottish Omnibuses on its overnight Scotland–London services; these were cleaned and refuelled at Victoria garage for many years.

In the main garage above SRTs briefly appeared, but were soon replaced by RTs, with RTLs replacing them in 1959. RMs arrived in 1964 and the RTLs departed in 1966. DMSs arrived in 1972 and lasted until 1977. Postwar STDs had lasted at Victoria until 1953, when with route 77 they were moved to Stockwell because

Above:
Victoria was also used as a venue for press events involving buses. Here the first Daimler Fleetline, with its 'Londoner' name writ large on the side, is besieged by a horde of pressmen. *Bill Godwin*

of Victoria's increasing problems in obtaining staff — a portent for the future, perhaps. Four of the STLs allocated for Festival of Britain services had been allocated here in 1951, working a route to the South Bank.

The pioneering Red Arrow route, the 500, worked from the garage from its introduction in April 1966, using Strachans-bodied AEC Merlins of the XMS class; the X stood for experimental, the S for standee. They were ousted from 1968 by their MBA successors, which in turn were quite soon replaced with later MBAs with high driving positions. But it is ironic that, while ordinary Merlins were all withdrawn by the end of 1976, those on Red Arrow duties — surely the hardest work — survived until May 1981, when they were replaced by Leyland Nationals of the LS class. The Red Arrow network grew, of course, from its original beginnings, though not all routes were operated by Victoria.

Another development came when the minibus era arrived in the provinces, with high-frequency routes operated by small buses apparently being very successful and winning back lost traffic. LT's hierarchy decided to try a Central London route and inaugurated the C1 (Westminster–Kensington), using OV-class Optare CityPacers, from October 1986. Though the idea might have been successful, the route never paid its way and for a time a premium fare was tried, with even Travelcard holders having to pay extra. The combination of MPs and influential people living on or near the route and defending it ultimately defeated LT, which dropped plans to withdraw it. It was worked from the basement at Victoria garage, which acquired its own garage code, GB. Other midibus routes were also introduced and operated from there; it became known as Central London Midibuses.

But the tendering regime struck a harsh blow when route 19, worked from Victoria, was awarded to Kentish

Above:
An impressive amount of overhead wiring is visible in this 1960 view of the exterior of the large Walthamstow depot,
viewed from the entrance gate. *John Gillham*

Bus. The removal of this route left Victoria with a large
amount of empty space, and put up the 'parking' cost
per bus per year for vehicles still based there to over
£5,300 — nearly double the cost per vehicle at other
garages. Closure was the answer. Other Routemaster-
operated routes were moved to the Red Arrow base at
Waterloo (the 11) and to Chelverton Road, Putney
(the 22). Weekend operation of the 11s (with one-
person buses) moved to Stockwell, which together with
Putney gained the rest of former GM operations from
June or July 1993. Midibuses from the basement GB
operation were moved to a new midibus base in Hester
Road, Battersea, which opened in June 1993 (initially
as an outstation to GB) operating MAs (Alexander-
bodied Mercedes-Benz midibuses) and MRLs (long-
wheelbase Optare MetroRiders). The base was opposite
the main part of the old LT Battersea garage.

After standing empty for some time, Victoria garage
was demolished in 2000 for work to begin on building
housing, shops and a supermarket on the site.

The garage was used not only for operational purposes but also by LT as the most convenient location
for press conferences to display new buses or for other
purposes. The first of its DMS Daimler Fleetlines was
unveiled there, while a perhaps more notable event was
the unveiling just before Christmas 1966 of FRM1.

WALTHAMSTOW (WW)
Chingford Road

In 1904 Walthamstow Urban District Council acquired
a site for a car shed for its new electric tramway system
which opened in June 1905. The original shed contained eight tracks, each for four trams, but increases in
the fleet in 1920 led to an extension with three more
tracks in an unpretentious addition, built mainly in
corrugated iron, that contrasted strongly with the
impressive 1904 office block adjoining the entrance.

Conversion to trolleybuses came in stages, with 27
starting work in October 1936, more in January 1937,
and the final stage in June 1937. However, the depot was
still connected to tram tracks so that redundant trams
could continue to be broken up in the yard behind.

The depot had a capacity of 107 trolleybuses, and in
1950 its scheduled requirement was for 99. Conversion
for buses was again in stages, though only two this time;
that in February 1960 required an allocation of 45
RMs, with a further 44 following in the April.

The opening of the Victoria Line of the Underground
to Walthamstow in 1968 brought a new route system to
the area, with the garage being allocated new MBs and
MBSs. From early 1974 DMSs started to arrive and the
following year replaced the MBs and MBSs. The last

Above:
Inside Walthamstow a new Jaco prototype automatic underfloor chassis cleaner is demonstrated. *Author's collection*

RMs left in 1981 and the garage became entirely one-person-operated, but Ts then began to replace the DMSs and ultimately became the only type in the garage.

Unfortunately the garage was part of the unsuccessful Forest District, where new route tenders were won on the basis of staff accepting new pay and conditions, which they refused. The tenders were then re-awarded to other operators, and the garage closed in November 1991. For a time it was used as a vehicle store, with (temporarily) surplus Titans being stored there along with Routemasters destined for Kentish Bus. It was sold for redevelopment in 1994.

WALWORTH (WL)
Camberwell New Road
(with an exit also to Camberwell Road)

This garage was originally the LCC's Camberwell tram depot, built on part of a site originally acquired by the London Tramways Company in 1891. It had a capacity for 135 bogie cars, having opened for the operation of

electric trams in October 1905. It was also the scene of the first experiments with conduit current collection.

To avoid confusion with Camberwell bus garage just across the road, the depot changed its name to Walworth in July 1950, when buses, trams and trolleybuses were merged into Central Road Services.

The depot had been badly damaged in World War 2, with 19 trams totally destroyed. In January 1951 it was still putting out a total of 101 trams on six different routes. Despite the partial demolition of the depot during the war, which might have been thought to simplify preparation for rebuilding, it was by no means ready for bus operation, though the new office block and staff quarters facing Camberwell New Road was complete. However, filling in the inspection pits provided sufficient space for parking about 60 buses. There were 50-plus RTLs for routes 176, 176A and 184 on the fifth stage of the tram conversion scheme in October 1951, plus a further 32 for the 185 which were worked by Walworth but nominally operated by (and parked at and serviced by) Camberwell garage opposite. The next stage of the changeover gave Walworth an

Above:
It was not until the trams had moved out that work could really get underway at Walworth (the former Camberwell tram depot) for conversion and rebuilding for buses. But the open parking area is being used, mainly to store STLs to be used in the last replacement stage in July 1952. *John Gillham*

Below:
An RTW is prominent on the forecourt of Walworth bus garage, another of London's modern garages to have a chequered career. It closed, reopened, closed again and was then used for a time by Londonlinks. *Kevin Lane*

allocation of 16 RTLs for route 36A, which it took over from Camberwell. The new garage was finally completed in 1954.

The RTLs were joined by RTWs in 1958 after service cuts generally allowed the wide buses to be allocated to routes 45 and 176. RMs replaced them in 1965, and RTs replaced the RTLs in 1966. MBAs were allocated for new Red Arrow routes in 1968, ultimately being replaced by LSs in 1981. DMSs and/or DMs also worked between 1971 and 1982; in the latter year Titans arrived to work with the RMs and LSs until closure in November 1985, when most of the work passed to Camberwell.

Although it never operated the type in service, for a time the garage stored withdrawn XA-class Leyland Atlanteans until they were shipped to Hong Kong in 1973.

Following closure of Victoria and Ash Grove, Walworth was reopened in 1987, acting as a Red Arrow base until the Waterloo site was ready. A further reopening occurred in the 1990s, when the Londonlinks operation based a number of tendered services here. Subsequently the Cowie Group undertook a major restructuring which saw operations at Walworth run down and then closed in August 1997, with routes transferred to Norwood, Cambridge Heath and Battersea.

WEST GREEN (WG)
Willow Walk, off West Green Road, N15

West Green was opened in late 1922 by B. G. D. Cosgrove, working originally with two buses from premises at Willow Walk owned by A. T. Bennett & Co on the 29 route and using the fleetname 'Admiral'. In the following year Bennett himself also began using buses from here. After buying a number of Straker-Squires, Bennett changed to Dennis. In 1925 he bought six dark blue-liveried, 26-seat Dodson-bodied Dennis 2½-ton normal-control chassis, which were some of London's first buses to run on pneumatic tyres. They worked on the 280 (Finsbury–Enfield). The following year the route (by now renumbered 538) gained new, slightly larger Dennis E-type single-deckers seating 30. These too had Dodson bodies, but the chassis were the first in London to be fitted with four-wheel brakes. In 1927 Bennett formed the London Public Omnibus Company, with its headquarters at the garage; the fleet built up to over 230 buses — not all kept at West Green! But hopes of a company of a size able to stand up to the LGOC were dashed when the LGOC took over in March 1928 and absorbed the business in December 1929, though Public was not actually wound up until a few months later.

The garage was the last to operate NS buses, and its remaining four, scheduled for operation on peaktime-only route 166 last ran on the evening of 30 November 1937 — an event that achieved some coverage in the press. By the outbreak of war the garage was running ST and Q types. Conversion to diesel-engined LTs took place in November 1939. In 1946 there were over 50 LTs, while the single-deckers were still Qs for route 233. When the hired Tilling Group Bristol double-deckers arrived in London, West Green was the only garage to put its entire allocation on to a single route, with 15 workings all on the combined 144/144A; it also operated some of the Bristols on Sundays — again, probably the only garage to do so. When new RTWs were received for the 144/144A late in 1949, some of the Bristols moved away, but eight moved on to the 144B for little more than a month before new RTLs were received. Half of the remaining Bristols then departed, while the other four moved again, spending about three months on route 29 before finally going to their owners. Later, in 1961, route 29 was again to have a short-lived type allocation, with five RMs being used for just a few months; West Green was not the major garage providing buses for the 29. It was, incidentally, only the second garage to receive RTLs, and kept them until it closed.

By 1952 requirements were met entirely by nearly 60 RTLs plus over 20 Qs. This changed little over the next few years, save that RFs replaced the Qs on the 233. In 1959 it became possible to double-deck the 233, but by then LT was beginning to seek ways of economising; although West Green was an average-sized garage with, in 1961, a peak requirement for 65 buses, nearby Wood Green (converted from trolleybus operation in November 1961) had spare capacity, so West Green closed in early January 1962, with its allocations on routes 29, 144, 217, 231 and 233 all moving there, while the 29A went to Palmers Green and the 171 to Tottenham.

WEST HAM (WH)
Greengate Street, West Ham

West Ham Corporation's new electric tram depot was built with style and panache in the days when municipalities took great pride in what they were creating. From the roof, it was said, there was an extensive view across the River Thames, and the Crystal Palace towers could be seen on a clear day. All that was back in October 1906 (and, of course, the Crystal Palace towers were demolished in the late 1930s). The splendid new depot replaced a temporary shed, and was able to accommodate 90 cars, with space for an extension for another 40. There were workshops and offices and a recreation room with a piano. In 1912 a Cedes-Stoll rail-less vehicle was demonstrated at the depot.

Conversion of West Ham depot for trolleybus operation began in 1936, with its first trolleybuses running in June 1937. But it was a protracted changeover, with the final trolleybuses not replacing the last trams in East London until June 1940. That also was the last replacement of trams by trolleybuses. West Ham was a very large depot, with a peak-hour requirement of 143 trolleybuses in 1955. But for some time after the trolleybuses had been replaced the motor-bus allocation was to be even greater.

Left:
Part of the parking area and main garage is visible in this picture of West Ham garage taken in 1988. The roundel on the wall reads 'LONDON BUSES' rather than 'LONDON TRANSPORT'.
Kevin Lane

Conversion of the depot entailed installation of four fuelling islands at the entrance, and six 5,000gal fuel tanks outside the building, along one side. There was a Februat washer, and the former trolleybus pits were adapted for bus use. Inside the main building there was parking space for 186 buses.

The first part of changeover to buses occurred in November 1959, when 15 RMs entered service. In a second stage in February 1960 another 55 RMs arrived, which still left 60 scheduled trolleybuses. The final stage (actually the sixth stage of the whole trolleybus conversion programme) came in April 1960, when West Ham gained another 61 RMs. But it was not quite as simple as that, because at the same time Forest Gate bus garage closed and its workings on the 25, totalling 68 RTs (and their crews), moved in. That was the first major mix of RMs and RTs in the same garage. It also made West Ham LT's second-largest garage, only New Cross running a greater number of buses. In 1966 the total bus requirement was 162, though by this time RTLs had replaced RTs, and RMLs were allocated as well as RMs.

The RMLs were to vanish in 1972, but returned in 1976 and stayed on until 1982. MBSs worked from the garage from 1969 to 1975 and SMSs from 1971 to 1979. DMS-type Daimler Fleetlines operated from 1971 to 1982, while the DM version for crew operation worked in 1978/9. RMs lasted until 1985, but since 1982 Titans had arrived in increasing numbers. LSs first came in 1979 and grew in numbers after Poplar garage closed in November 1985; at the same time the garage's fleet became entirely one-person-operated.

Although its total allocation had declined over the years, West Ham was still a busy garage in 1987, with a peak requirement of 113 buses. But steady losses were to follow for London Buses' East London routes generally, although in December 1991 the garage gained 20 new Scania double-deckers for use on four of the D-numbered services serving Docklands. However, the garage was also costly to maintain, needed repairs 'which East London could not afford, and the company has plenty of garage space anyway', so it closed in October 1992, with its work passing to Bow, Leyton and Upton Park.

—③—

Garages used by London Buses or former London Buses companies after privatisation

This chapter details garages in use with London Buses subsidiaries upon privatisation, most of which are still operational, as well as bases opened/taken over subsequently. Also included are the premises used by East Thames Buses, Transport for London's directly owned operation.

ARRIVA LONDON NORTH/NORTH EAST

Leaside was bought by Cowie Group plc in September 1994; the group subsequently renamed itself Arriva, with Leaside becoming Arriva London North 1998. At the same time, the former Grey-Green operation became Arriva London North East.

BARKING (BR/DX★)
Ripple Road

Grey-Green acquired this site in Ripple Road to meet a pressing need for more accommodation for its expanding bus fleet. It built a modern repair facility on the site, which came into use in March 1992 (though building work was incomplete) to house vehicles for four North East London routes won from Thamesway.

Dix Coaches was a Grey-Green subsidiary that had been running LT routes in East London from its bus depot in Dagenham, and these duly transferred to the new base in Barking. Although the Dix name has long since been abandoned, these origins are reflected in the DX code used for what is now an Arriva London North East depot.

Including school routes, Barking had a scheduled requirement in late 1997 of just over 50 buses, but by 2001 this had increased to nearly 70.

CLAPTON (CT)
(formerly Hackney)
Bohemia Place, Mare Street, Hackney

As well as having seen four different forms of traction — horse and electric trams, trolleybus and motor bus —

Clapton demonstrates the ups and downs of bus operation in the last part of the 20th century. Closed in 1987, by 1999 it had a scheduled requirement for well over 100 buses.

The depot site had been bought in 1882 by the North Metropolitan Tramways Company for its Mare Street car shed. After the LCC took over the horse trams in 1906 it had a new depot built to house electric trams; this opened in 1909. Conversion for trolleybus operation followed in 1939, with some introduced in September that year, and the last trams going in November. By 1940 part of Bohemia Place had been taken over and buildings demolished to allow better access to the depot. The name was changed from Hackney in 1950 to avoid confusion with the bus garage in Well Street (H).

Work began in 1958 to convert the depot for motor buses. A washing machine replaced the gantry used for hand-washing trolleybuses, a sprinkler system was installed, the vacuum-cleaning plant was modernised and fuelling islands and three 5,000gal fuel tanks were installed. The parking area provided room for 90 buses. Trolleybus replacement took place in April 1959, this being only the second stage to be implemented, so 67 RTLs were allocated.

RTs replaced the RTLs in 1967 and remained until 1974; the first RMs arrived in 1969. DMSs appeared in 1972 and were replaced by Ts in 1982. Ms also put in an appearance, but from 1987 just a few RMs and Ts remained. The garage closed in August 1987, most work transferring to Ash Grove, which was not far away. In the later years of trolleybus operation the peak scheduled requirement had totalled 68 vehicles, but the requirement for buses was generally around 60.

Closure was not to last long, and in May 1989 the

garage reopened, initially to accommodate a fleet of MRLs from Walthamstow to work route 236, with maintenance still undertaken at Walthamstow. But things built up steadily after that, helped partly by the subsequent closure of Ash Grove.

By May 1994 it was working route 38, with a scheduled requirement for 37 RMLs and the 106 (transferred from Ash Grove) with 11 Ms. Better was to come, when the 253 — probably London's most frequent route — was moved from Stamford Hill, with a need for 48 Ms or Ls. Summer 1998 saw a liquid petroleum gas (lpg)-powered DAF SB220/Plaxton Prestige single-decker work a three-month trial on the (double-deck) 253. More significantly, in November the same year London's first four low-floor double-deckers entered full-time service from Clapton on route 242; they were the first of many DAF DB250RS(LF) double-deckers with Alexander ALX400 bodywork to be bought by Arriva for its London operations. By 2001 the RML requirement for the 38 had risen to 41, and there were 18 DLAs on the 242 and 48 Ls on the 253 — 117 buses in all.

EDMONTON (EM/BC⋆)
Edmonton Wharf, off Harbet Road, Lea Valley Trading Estate

The former London Suburban base at Edmonton Wharf reopened in September 1997 as a depot for Arriva-owned County Bus. A year later the garage and most of these operations and the Leaside Travel work was all transferred to Arriva London North. Operations include several schooldays services.

ENFIELD (E)
Southbury Road and Harts Way, Ponders End

This garage was built by the LGOC in 1927 and then handed over to the London Public Omnibus Company for it to use shortly after LGOC gained financial control in March 1928. London Public was finally wound up in April 1930. Further land was later acquired to allow a bus stand to be provided on the forecourt, and this was subsequently also used as a trolleybus terminus.

A major updating scheme took place in the mid-

1980s, with an official opening in October 1984. Some £6¾ million was spent on modernising the garage and extending it over the site of a disused factory. As improved it had space for 106 buses; before the work began the allocation had been 68 buses. More recently it has become rather more than just a bus garage, being also the home of Arriva's Enfield Accident Repair Centre. Much early work there was concentrated on remedial work on Metrobuses, but the current output is not merely for Arriva companies but also for other operators. Accident repair work includes re-roofing buses damaged in low-bridge incidents, while repairing or replacing floors on double-deckers are frequent tasks. Recent work for Arriva has included refurbishment of Ls, including fitment of new gearboxes, and RMLs.

Over the years the garage has operated a vast number of different types. In August 1939 it ran STLs, single-deck LTs, Ts, Cs and DAs. By the end of 1945 it had

some 81 Gs and at one time in the early postwar period was running RTs, RTLs, STDs, Gs, Ts and TDs. The STDs were prewar buses replacing some of the Gs. Allocations of RTLs and RTWs (from 1949) were replaced from 1952 by RTs, which lasted until 1978. RMs arrived in 1968 and DMSs in 1972. From 1981 onwards Ms replaced the DMSs and ultimately formed the bulk of the fleet. After the TD type went in 1953 there were no more single-deckers until RFs arrived in 1966 for route 121, which had been operated for a time in the 1950s by the only postwar Guy double-decker, G436.

LT's first minibus service, the W9 (Southgate–Enfield Town) began in September 1972, worked by Strachans-bodied Ford Transits (FSs), initially for an experimental period of six months. Bristol LHSs (BSs) replaced them in 1976 and were in turn succeeded by standard-length LHs (BLs) in 1981, but the route passed to Eastern National in an early stage of tendering, in 1985. Larger single-deckers operated by Enfield were MBSs and

MBs, then SMSs. Both RFs and SMSs left in 1976. RMs did not arrive until quite late, but then stayed some years. By 1994 Ms formed the entire allocation, some 73 being scheduled. By 2001 the total allocation was slightly higher, with 56 new low-floor DAF DB250 double-deckers carrying Alexander (DLAs) or Plaxton (DLPs) bodywork, plus 18 Plaxton Pointer-bodied Dennis Darts (LDRs) and five less-common Northern Counties-bodied Darts (DRNs).

PALMERS GREEN (AD)
Regents Avenue, off Green Lanes, Palmers Green

The LGOC opened its garage in Palmers Green in July 1912, primarily to service the bus route to the town that it had begun the previous year in competition with the electric trams of the Metropolitan Electric Tramways Company. The buses ran right through to Central London and the MET then proposed putting on its own bus services to counter the competition. Negotiations ended with the LGOC operating the blue-liveried buses of the MET.

Just before the outbreak of World War 2 the garage's allocation was entirely STL. In contrast, when the garage received RTs in 1951 it became the only garage to have had an allocation of all four postwar standard types of double-decker from new: RT, RTL, RTW and SRT. However, none of these buses could go in the garage until its roof had been raised, by 10in. This was achieved by jacking up the whole structure by one inch at a time at 40 different places — a process which took 20 weeks.

The allocation of SRTs (for route 34) was in April 1949, but complaints of poor brakes by the drivers led to a test in Longmoor Avenue, East Barnet, where a bus with a simulated full load was unable to stop within a reasonable distance. All except one already-modified SRT were taken out of service and replaced by buses from all over the fleet including ST1, early petrol STLs and one of the STLs with ST-style bodies. The SRTs duly returned to service following modifications, but all were subsequently removed to garages with less-arduous routes.

RTs lasted at the garage until 1978 but were supplemented by RMs from 1969. One-person operation of route 212 in 1971 brought in a few RFs, replaced in 1976 by SMSs and in the following year by DMSs. Modernisation of the garage began in the early 1970s and was completed in 1974, by which time there was a maximum scheduled requirement for 60 buses.

From October 1981 Ms began arriving to work the one-person-operated routes. Something more interesting was a Volvo Citybus with an accumulator storage system for converting the energy generated in braking so that it could be used for accelerating. The bus, numbered C1, ran on the 102 (Golders Green–Chingford) from July 1986 to September 1987. By this time the vehicle requirement at the garage was for fewer than 50 buses, all Ms apart from 17 RMs for the 29. It improved slightly thereafter, with an all-M requirement of 51 in 1994. By 2001 the figure had improved marginally again, with a scheduled need for 30 Metrobuses for three routes, eight Volvo Citybuses with Alexander bodies (VAs) for the 125 and a more impressive 17 low-floor DAF/Alexanders (DLAs) for the 329.

Below:
Cones mark off a small part of Palmers Green garage for a Metrobus in Arriva's training livery to be used for basic driver instruction. *Author*

STAMFORD HILL (SF)
Rookwood Road, Stamford Hill

Stamford Hill was built as an LCC tram depot 'for the electrical working of the first section of the northern tramways of the LCC', according to the tender documents. It came into operation in February 1907.

Alterations made to the depot for the trolleybuses were rather less drastic than at other depots, and trolleybuses began running from it in February 1939. They lasted until 1961, when in July the garage received 55 RMs. That was not quite the whole story, as only 48 trolleybuses had been operated in the previous year, making the site rather under-utilised. It was decided that Stamford Hill was in an ideal position for efficient scheduling and that it would be better to cut down on the bus use of Edmonton (part of which was later used to store tunnel components for the Victoria Line) and add a further bus route to Stamford Hill. Unfortunately that route, the 253, was in an earlier phase of the conversion scheme, so was temporarily based at Edmonton and did not move into Stamford Hill until October. Capacity of the trolleybus depot had been 97, but even by 1950 only 66 were being operated, the figure subsequently falling considerably.

Above and below:
For a short time Stamford Hill operated both trolleybuses and motor buses. Both types are seen making use of the traverser; the curtain to its right hides building work. *(both) Author*

From December 1965 the garage took part in a series of comparison trials involving RMLs and XAs. RMLs were introduced on to the 67 and ran until July the following year, when they were exchanged with XAs from Highgate. Having arrived, the XAs remained until 1969/70. RMLs reappeared in 1970, and DMSs the following year, with DMs following in 1974. But in 1980 the DMs were ousted by refurbished RCLs. These were former Green Line vehicles which had been handed over to London Country in 1970 and had been bought back by LT when they were being disposed of. The vehicles were overhauled, had their platform doors removed and were reupholstered, but the generous seat spacing was retained, so these 30ft-long vehicles provided just 64 seats. They were normally restricted to route 149 (which was worked also by Edmonton) and lasted until 1984.

RMLs had left in 1981, but came back in 1986, joining Ms which had arrived in 1982 as DMS replacements. In May 1994 Stamford Hill had a total requirement for 70 buses, all double-deckers, there being 32 Ms, 36 Ls and two Ts. But the garage closed in May 1995, with displaced buses and crews moving to Enfield, Tottenham, Clapton and Wood Green. It reopened the following year as the home of the Leaside Travel fleet and Leaside's driver-training fleet — about 55 vehicles all told. But most of the training fleet moved to Clapton and Tottenham in late 1997, while the 26 vehicles of Leaside Travel passed to County Bus at Edmonton. Since March 2000 the garage has been officially 'mothballed'.

TOTTENHAM (AR)
Philip Lane, off High Road, Tottenham

Built on a site previously occupied by sawmills, Tottenham garage opened in July 1913 to run services for Tramways (MET) Omnibus Company, which had been set up by the Metropolitan Electric Tramways Company to run buses to augment and feed its tram routes. It began with a fleet of gearless Daimlers, which were requisitioned on the outbreak of World War 1. The garage was passed to AEC on loan from 1917 until June 1919, when it reopened as a bus garage. In the meantime MET and the LGOC had come to an agreement and the garage had been bought by the LGOC. The acute shortages after the war saw some of the LGOC's lorry-buses worked from it.

In summer 1939 the fleet comprised STs, STLs and LTs. During World War 2 it became the first garage to receive an allocation of utility Gs, from December 1942; by June 1943 it had 43 of them. They ousted LTs which by November 1940 had replaced all the STLs. In the early postwar period Tottenham was the last garage with an official schedule of STs for one route, the 67; while many other garages still operated them, they were usually used to augment other types and cover shortages. The 12 scheduled STs were replaced by STLs in January 1950, and they in turn were replaced by RTLs later that year. The garage also became the first in London to run 8ft-wide buses, on route 41 in May 1949 — starting with just two RTWs. Drivers were each allowed three days for type training because of the extra width.

Below:
Tottenham has always been a busy garage and for a time had an entirely double-deck allocation. Here one of the later Metrobuses stands alongside a Routemaster. *D. J. Fitch/Kevin Lane collection*

The 76/34B allocation had been the first route to run the Gs, but it was decided to replace them, initially with STLs and then with RTLs — a decision probably influenced by the forthcoming Festival of Britain in 1951 and thoughts that the spartan Gs might not present the right image on a route passing the main Festival site at Waterloo.

New single-deckers for the garage were TDs, replaced by RFs in 1958, which lasted until route 236 moved to Dalston garage in 1971. No more single-deckers were to work from the garage for some 30 years, until, from February 2001, 11 PDLs (Dennis Dart SLF/Plaxton Pointer 2s) were allocated for route W4, newly won on tender.

RMs began to arrive in 1962, ousting the RTWs in 1965, and stayed until the late 1980s. Evaluation tests on the 76 route saw the RTWs ousted by RMLs (plus three RMs for workings which included the 34B), with XAs (Leyland Atlanteans) arriving in 1966 and staying until 1970. A more notable arrival was FRM1, which worked at the garage from 1967 to 1969.

From 1971 some RMLs reappeared (having left when the XAs arrived) and worked on route 243, lasting (on and off) until 1985. They reappeared once again in 1986 for route 73 and were still working it in 2001. Meanwhile DMSs arrived in 1972 and stayed for 10 years before being replaced by Ms.

The dock area of the garage was modernised in 1972, and further modernisation work took place in 1985/6. In October 1999 there was an official opening of an extension to the garage — a rare event these days! It also included transfer of Arriva London's driver-training department and its buses to the garage, leading to the closure and mothballing of Stamford Hill (SF) in 2000.

Allocations at the garage had steadily dropped over the years, from 156 scheduled buses in 1952 to 124 in late 1976 and 87 in early 1987. In 1994 the total was 90 (45 Ms and 45 RMLs), but by mid-2001 it was much busier, with 134 buses. There were 20 Ms, 48 RMLs, 24 VAs (Alexander-bodied Volvo Citybuses), 33 DLAs (low-floor DAFs with Alexander ALX400 bodies) and the nine new single-deckers mentioned earlier.

WOOD GREEN (WN)
High Road and River Park Road, Wood Green

Three special electric tramcars from Wood Green depot took directors and their guests on an inaugural tour of the routes on the opening day of the new system of the Metropolitan Electric Tramways Company — 22 July 1904. The company had acquired the depot in 1902 from the North Metropolitan Tramways Company, which in turn had bought it from the receiver to the North London Tramways Company, which had run horse and steam trams. The Northern Metropolitan had undertaken not to run the steam trams again but to substitute horse-drawn cars.

The shed and stables were transformed into a modern depot to hold 62 cars. By 1908 it had been extended to house 87, and further additions were made in 1912. The depot was almost completely remodelled again in 1937/8 ready for trolleybuses to replace the trams. The new fleet began operating in May 1938 from

Above:
Wood Green garage is well situated for operating purposes, opposite a tube station and by an important road junction. Here a Routemaster pulls out to take up the running on route 29. *Kevin Lane*

Left:
Trolleybuses stand over the smart docking area at the west end of Wood Green depot, not long before motor buses took over. *John Gillham*

Above:
More than the usual mix of vehicles can be seen in this 1967 line-up at Wood Green. Foremost is what became known as RT1, then the engineering training unit with RT1's body mounted on a postwar chassis. The GS on the right was used for civil-defence purposes. *Author*

a depot with a capacity of 108. In 1950 the scheduled requirement in was for 98 trolleybuses.

The depot was adapted for motor buses in 1960/1, with a partial conversion in April 1961 and the remainder of the routes in November. There had been pressure on LT to withdraw trolleybus route 629 earlier than planned to allow a big new one-way traffic scheme at Tottenham Court Road to be introduced; this was reluctantly agreed to, and 46 RMs were allocated to Wood Green. The main part of the changeover took place as originally planned in November, when Wood Green received a further 37 RMs. No sooner had all these RMs settled in than in January 1962 West Green bus garage was closed, with most of its work moving here.

The first of the much-publicised bus service reshaping schemes was introduced at Wood Green in September 1968, about a year after it was expected to start. Some 40 MBSs were allocated to the garage for the new flat-fare, one-person-operated routes, which were numbered W1 to W6. A few RMLs were operated in 1970/1 and DMSs arrived early in 1973 for further one-person conversions, and the following year they ousted the RTs and later the MBSs. Ms were allocated from mid-1981 and eliminated DMSs. In 1975 some DMs (crew-operated DMSs) had

arrived and lasted until 1982; they had worked mainly on the 29, which was one of those busy routes which subsequently reverted to Routemaster operation.

In its later trolleybus days the depot had a peak requirement for 89: by the mid-1960s, swelled by the work moved in from West Green, the bus total was 113, but it gradually fell, to 89 by early 1987. By May 1994 things had stabilised, with an allocation of 77 Ms and 13 DRLs (9m Dennis Darts). A notable event in July 1998 was the operation of the prototype low-floor DAF/Alexander double-decker, which did odd journeys on both the 144 and the 29. By mid-2001 the garage had more than 50 of the type scheduled on three routes, all being DAFs with Alexander ALX400 bodies. Other scheduled double-deck operations require some 40 Ms. Until 2001, route 263 was worked with step-entrance DAF DB250s with distinctive Northern Counties Palatine II bodies — a rare type in London — but this route has since been lost on re-tender and the buses transferred away. Striking newcomers later in the year were Wright-bodied Volvo B7TLs — Wright's first double-deckers. Some 21 9.8m Dennis Dart/Plaxtons complete the total requirement for nearly 130 buses — a big increase on that of a few years ago.

ARRIVA LONDON SOUTH

South London was the last company to be privatised, and was bought by Cowie Group (later Arriva) in December 1994, with the purchase being ratified subsequently. The company was renamed Arriva London South in 1998.

BATTERSEA (BA)
Hester Road

A yard adjacent to the closed Battersea garage is used (as an outstation to Brixton Garage) for Routemasters on route 19.

BEDDINGTON FARM, CROYDON (BF/CN★)
Beddington Farm Road, off Purley Way, Croydon

This depot is one of the few modern, purpose-built, mainly open-air depots in the London area. It was opened in December 1990 by London & Country Greenway, which was the short-lived name for the eastern section of London Country South West. It ran 73 vehicles at the opening, with space for 120 in the open parking area, and had cost £6.1 million. The main facilities included a covered body shop and maintenance area with pits and lifts, a steam-cleaning bay and a vehicle wash with recycling facilities. It was designed to replace the garages at Godstone and Chelsham, and at the time of opening worked four tendered routes, plus four more of London & Country's own which ran into Croydon. It also had outstations at Newington Butts, of 18 buses for route 78 (Forest Hill–Shoreditch), and of

eight at the Kentish Bus garage at Dunton Green for route 320 (Westerham–Biggin Hill).

Beddington Farm was to have a chequered career thanks to various reorganisations, and would become a Londonlinks depot when non-LT work moved away. After becoming a part of Arriva that ran blue-liveried buses, it was officially transferred to Arriva London South in October 1999 with six routes, its 57 buses variously painted green, blue or red.

BRIXTON (BN)
Streatham Hill

A depot for the cable trams which ran up Brixton Hill had been built on this site in 1892. Between 1904 and 1906 it was rebuilt by the LCC for use by its electric trams, the premises being known thereafter as Telford Avenue depot. In 1913 an extension was added on the south side, on the other side of the road owned by the Metropolitan Water Board — and of a large-capacity water-main.

When the garage was reconstructed from 1949 (it took until 1953 to complete) extensive works were necessary to bury the main, so that there could be one complete building, rather than the two (with a link) of tram days. To enable work to get underway, many trams were moved to the nearby Brixton Hill tram depot. Known as Brixton North, its use ended in January 1954, buses having been parked there latterly. Subsequently sold to a car-sales company, the building was still standing in 2001.

The first part of the changeover took place in January 1951, but the buses had to be housed in a car park

Above:
The large and mainly open-air Beddington Farm depot in Croydon has a range of buildings and offices along one side of the large site. The rest of the open area is spacious enough for Arriva to be able to stage its own driving competition heat for London Bus Driver of the Year contenders. *Maurice Doggett*

Above:
This is the larger (north) shed of the former LCC Telford Avenue tram depot, pictured in 1950.
The south shed, off to the right, was on the other side of a large water main. *John Gillham*

behind Streatham Hill Theatre; facilities here included a Guy chassis with fuel tank mounted on it, and other Gs used as offices and staff rest room. The last trams ran from the depot in April 1951, by which time the garage had an allocation of 90 RTs. Between 1963 and 1965, RTLs and RTWs ousted the RTs, which returned from 1965 and finally departed in 1976. The garage became the last to run RTWs — on three routes, all finishing in mid-May 1966; RMs replaced them.

In January 1971 the garage became one of the first two to operate DMSs, on route 95, which was converted from crewed RMs. Some Ms arrived in November 1984, but DMSs continued to form a large part of the allocation. Among the Metrobuses were a batch of 22 with Cummins engines. By 1994 the garage was running 25 RMs and 22 RMLs on routes 159 and 137 respectively, and these allocations continue with little change in 2001. The only other vehicles in 1994 were 28 Ms, making a total allocation of 75. The 2001 total of 92 buses was an improvement and included 10 DLAs (low-floor DAF/Alexander ALX400), 17 Ls (ECW-bodied Olympians) and 16 DDLs (Dennis Dart SLFs with Plaxton Pointer 2 bodies). Late in 2001 the garage received the first production DWL-class DAF SB120/Wright Cadet single-deckers bought by Arriva London.

Right:
The water main was lowered and enclosed to provide one large site for the new Brixton bus garage. The architecture of the office block, seen here, was in typical 1950s style. *Gerald Mead*

Above:
Croydon garage had been substantially rebuilt after World War 2. Here a Leyland Olympian on route 68 edges out into the busy Brighton Road, taking precedence over a Fleetline on the same route. *Author*

CROYDON (TC)

Brighton Road, Napier Road and Crunden Road, South Croydon

The LGOC built Croydon garage, but when completed it was handed over to Thomas Tilling under an agreement between the two operators and opened for traffic in January 1916, with 40 TTA1s (Tilling's original type of petrol-electric double-decker) and their crews moved from Tilling's Lewisham garage. Strangely, TTA1s from Tilling's premises at Victory Place, Elephant & Castle, then moved to Lewisham in replacement.

The garage had its roof raised in the early 1930s to accommodate covered-top double-deckers. In August 1939 it was running single-deck LTs, and STs and STLs, many of the double-deckers being former Tilling buses. An unusual operation from September 1935 had been the use of three Gilfords transferred from the Country Area on one-man-operated route 203 — Purley (Old Lodge Lane)–Mitchley Avenue — which was subsidised by two house-building companies; Dennis Darts took over in April 1936.

The garage was completely burnt out in an air raid on the night of 10/11 May 1941, being first set alight and then used as a guide for other aircraft to drop their bombs. Four staff were killed in the bombing. The 56 buses destroyed included two Tilling STs, 22 Tilling STLs and three loaned Manchester Corporation Crossleys. The raid took place on a Saturday night/Sunday morning, but the garage ran a full service on the Monday with buses borrowed from 11 garages. Later in the war the garage was allocated a maximum of 27 STs towing producer-gas trailers; the buses were used on route 197, a route devoid of gradients. One is said to

have strayed on to the 59B to Old Coulsdon but failed to make it up the hill from Coulsdon.

Reconstruction of the garage was not finished until the mid-1950s. The garage was allocated just nine of the postwar all-Leyland STDs, which arrived late in 1946, to make a very minor dent in the ranks of the mainly petrol-engined STs and STLs at the garage. They did not stay long, soon moving to Loughton, but the garage would receive a sizeable allocation of postwar RTs late in 1947 and early in 1948. Variety was added with some of the hired Tilling Group K-type double-deckers, Croydon receiving some Eastern Counties examples. Ultimately RTs were to monopolise the garage until 1964, apart from the LT single-deckers and then RFs for route 234A. RMs arrived in 1964 and were joined in 1967 by RMLs, which went on to oust the RMs; however, the latter came back in 1970, the same year that a large batch of SMSs was allocated.

November 1969 saw an XA (experimental Leyland Atlantean/Park Royal) become LT's first one-person-operated double-decker, replacing an RF on the 233 (Roundshaw Estate–West Croydon). The actual bus was XA22, which would be the last of its type to operate, in March 1973; the XAs were all sold to China Motor Bus in Hong Kong. A more famous bus to work on the 233 was the sole rear-engined Routemaster, FRM1, which operated from the garage for a time. Another event of considerable interest was the hiring of 10 Southend Corporation Leyland PD3s with manual gearboxes for route 190 (Old Coulsdon–Thornton Heath) to help alleviate the chronic shortage of vehicles; these blue buses ran from September 1975 to February 1976, when RMs returned to the route.

When the XAs were sold in 1973 they were replaced

by DMSs on the 234, 234A and C-prefix flat-fare routes to New Addington. Almost 20 years later, DMS2438 was the last of the B20 'quiet' Fleetlines to operate in the fleet on scheduled work: it finished on 20 January 1993, though odd examples of the type lingered for a while for private-hire or other limited use.

In 1977 the RFs were replaced by BLs, which later gave way to LSs. Some Ms arrived in 1985, but moved on a couple of years later when a batch of Ls (Leyland Olympian/ECW) arrived. Closure of Elmers End in 1986 brought many route and vehicle changes, with Croydon losing its RMs but regaining LSs, and becoming an entirely one-person-operated garage. By 1994 the garage had become all-double-deck, 52 Ls and 57 Ms making 109 buses in all.

The garage went on to lose most of its Ls in favour of older Ms, but the balance eventually changed, with the last M moving out in 2001. It also gained some Dennis Darts, while a more interesting operation was of route TL1, which replaced the former Connex South Central train service between West Croydon and Wimbledon while Croydon Tramlink was being built. The route was worked mainly by DAF SB220s with Ikarus Citibus bodies — a rare type in large fleets. By mid-2001 there was a requirement for 30 Ls plus 45 low-floor DAF double-deckers (DLAs) and 22 of two different types of Dennis Dart/Plaxton (LDRs and DRLs).

NORWOOD (N)
Knights Hill, Ernest Avenue and Rotherschild Street, Norwood

Opened in March 1909 by the LGOC, Norwood garage was deep in tram territory. When the garage was being enlarged in 1925 *Tramway & Railway World* commented that 'the vehicles housed in this depot provided, on considerable portions of the route, more competition with LCC Tramways than is the case on any other tramway route'.

When the garage opened it had begun with G-type Straker-Squires derived from the London Road Car fleet, some of them still in the distinctive livery with 'Union Jack' fleetnames. By mid-1939 the garage was running a mix of LTs and STs. RTs had arrived from autumn 1950, but some STLs allocated for extra Festival of Britain services in 1951 were housed at the nearby Norwood tram depot that was soon to close. The first RMs arrived in 1964 and by 1970 were the sole type allocated up until closure for rebuilding in April 1981.

The buses and the staff then moved temporarily to the reopened Clapham, returning three years later to a new £5 million garage. Some Ms were allocated in 1985 but were replaced the following year by Ls. In March 1987 RMLs joined the RMs. Although Ls might be regarded as beyond the mid-life stage, one recent new contract was won on the basis of the Ls being refurbished — work which includes fitting new Voith gearboxes to replace the original Leyland units. A transfer of former Londonlinks operations by the Cowie Group in 1997 moved the 176 and 188 to Norwood, together with 36 Volvo Citybuses with distinctive East Lancs bodies to operate them; however, these buses subsequently moved elsewhere within the Arriva empire.

For many years the garage's maximum scheduled requirement varied between 74 and 65, but recent totals have been rather higher: mid-2001 schedules require 68 Ls (both unrefurbished and refurbished) and 25 low-floor Dennis Tridents with Alexander ALX400 bodies. Unusually for modern times, there are no single-deckers.

Below:
The unusual layout at the new Norwood garage placed the admin block high above an area where terminating buses can lay over. To the left can be seen the exit from the garage proper. *Author*

THORNTON HEATH (TH)
Whitehall Road, Thornton Heath

The first horse tramway in Croydon opened in October 1879 and operated from a small depot near Thornton Heath Pond. It was later rebuilt for Croydon Corporation's new electric trams, which began running in September 1901. Room was provided at first for 26 trams, but an extension the following year enlarged it to take 43 cars. It became the first tram depot to be closed in connection with the 1950-2 replacement programme, but actually shut long before any tram routes were converted, on 1 January 1950; its trams, staff and equipment all moved to Purley depot, which until recently had been overhauling trams.

Although rebuilding was not yet finished, buses were able to use the garage from the start of Stage 3 of the conversion programme in April 1951. It began with a complement of 54 RTs, for routes 109 and 190, but was designed to take up to 107 buses. By early 1953 it was providing up to 84 buses at peak periods, though by mid-1996 the figure had fallen to 69.

Garage design followed standard LT practice, with covered parking, pits and workshop, but there is also an open parking area behind the garage. Equipment included a central vacuum-cleaning plant, two Essex washers and underground fuel tanks. A separate two-storey office block and canteen faces the main London Road but has no entry from it.

RTs lasted at the garage until 1976, having been joined by RMs from 1962. DMSs replaced the RMs in 1971, but RMs returned in 1976, left again in 1978, and then came back in 1982, thereafter remaining until the garage became entirely one-person-operated in February 1987, with a fleet of DMSs. DMs also worked between 1978 and 1982, while SMSs were allocated between 1970 and 1980.

October 1989 saw the operation for a few months of SA1, a Scania N113/Alexander single-decker, on normally double-deck service 59 (Purley–Brixton). It was then swapped with Bromley garage for a DAF/Optare Delta for a few months, before returning for another spell to complete a year's operation with LT.

By 1994 the whole fleet had changed. Three routes were worked with Ls (ECW-bodied Leyland Olympians) while the trunk 109 and the X30 between them called for 47 buses, a mix mainly of Ls and Ms. Smaller buses comprised 10 early Dennis Darts plus seven Metroriders. Seven years later, Darts were still in evidence, including some longer versions; the 109 needed 24 buses, which were a mix of Ls and low-floor DAF double-deckers with Alexander ALX400 bodies of the DLA class. Also on strength, but soon to depart, were Six DLOs — low-floor DAF/Optare Spectra double-deckers which originated with Capital Logistics when it worked route 60.

EAST THAMES

Above:
East Thames is now a subsidiary of Transport for London.
Author

East Thames Buses was not a buy-out from London Transport in the 1990s but a new company set up by London Buses to take over bus operation in its own right from the receiver of former contractor Harris Bus. It began trading in 2000 using a garage still in LT ownership.

ASH GROVE (AG)
off Mare Street, Hackney

Old maps show part of the site of Ash Grove garage as a 'female refuge'. Today the garage has engulfed most of the former thoroughfare from which it takes its name, with only a minute remainder providing entry to the gates of the garage. It was the first of three new garages to open in 1981, the ceremony being completed when Dr David Quarmby, Managing Director (Buses) of LT, drove the official first bus into the garage. It cost over £3.5 million and came into use in the April. There was space for 140 buses under cover and another 30 in a yard to one side, plus extensive offices and car-parking space.

The roof is unusual in being carried by 10 triangular trusses each weighing 35 tons, said to be the largest of their type in the UK. They are supported on reinforced concrete columns around the perimeter of the building. Brickwork cladding rises to a height of 5m on the walls, with glazing above. The operations block is a three-storey building of curtain-walling and brick on a reinforced concrete frame.

Though Ash Grove is technically in Hackney, buses showed 'CAMBRIDGE HEATH Ash Grove Garage' on their blinds. The garage took over the work of the nearby Dalston and Hackney garages, each of which was about 70 years old, and on the day of its opening assumed Hackney's operation of Red Arrow routes 502 and 513, using brand-new LSs which had been stored

in the yard at Ash Grove pending entry into service. Unfortunately the garage soon acquired a reputation for militancy by a small proportion of its staff and also found itself in the London Forest operation which collapsed when staff refused to operate tenders it had won based on lower wages and changed working conditions. It closed in November 1991.

The garage reopened in May 1994 for use by Kentish Bus on some of that company's tendered London services, and continued in this role until February 1998. However, Kentish Bus never referred to it by its previous name; it was now known as Cambridge Heath.

The garage was also being used to store vehicles of the LT Museum fleet — those for which there was no room at Covent Garden — but these later moved to the Museum's new climate-controlled store at Acton Town.

Ash Grove reopened once again in March 2000, when LT itself, through new subsidiary East Thames Buses, took over from the receiver the services previously operated by Harris Bus; buses and staff are based here and at Belvedere. Later in 2000 the garage was also used to store Routemasters acquired from various sources and awaiting refurbishment as part of the plan by Transport for London to increase Routemaster operation in London. However, the East Thames fleet occupies only a modest part of the garage, and some of its offices and facilities are based in portable buildings within the main building.

A further development is the use of most of the parking area as a base for the LT tendered services operated by Hackney Community Transport. These include route 153, worked by a fleet of 11 Dennis Dart SLFs with Caetano Nimbus bodies, and a group of Mobility Bus routes in East and North London, worked by four unusual three-axle Fiat Ducatos with Rohill bodies with tail-lifts.

BELVEDERE (BV)
Butts Wharf, Crabtree Manor Way North, Belvedere

When East Thames Buses took over the buses and the running of the services formerly operated by Harris Bus (after the latter went into receivership) it also took over the base at Butts Wharf from which the routes south of the River Thames are operated.

As there are no engineering facilities at Butts Wharf, two drivers are employed at night to ferry buses to and from the Ash Grove garage for routine servicing and any other attention. Because double-deckers cannot use the Blackwall Tunnel, these have to take a long, indirect route through Central London. To eliminate this expensive operation, East Thames is buying from the United States a portable building containing a vehicle-servicing unit, which it plans to install at Butts Wharf.

Above:
Probably London Transport's most expensive garage, Ash Grove has had a chequered career and only recently reopened to a fleet of red London buses. On 24 April 1981 brand-new Leyland Nationals are lined up in the yard to start work on Red Arrow routes when the garage opens for business next morning. *John Gillham*

Below:
Though Ash Grove is home to most of the East Thames fleet, that fills only about one third of the space. In the later part of 2000 it was also used to store the Routemasters acquired by TfL from various sources before they went away for refurbishment. *Author*

FIRST CENTREWEST

CentreWest was the subject of a management/employee buy-out completed in September 1994. The company was subsequently acquired by FirstGroup plc.

ACTON (AT)
High Street, Acton by the junction with Gunnersbury Lane

Acton Tram Depot, as it is still called — even on the destination blinds of buses — is one of the most remarkable survivors from the early years of street-based public transport. It is the first depot to have been built in the Greater London area for electric tramway operation, even though for its first five years it was actually used for horse trams — there was a paddock behind it for them to graze. The depot was built for the London United Tramways and designed by a local architect of some ability. The building itself, a four-bay structure with arched pediments over the entrances, was — and is — of exceptionally strong construction. It has now been home to four forms of transport: horse tram, electric tram, trolleybus and — belatedly — motor bus.

Opened in 1896, it housed some 150 horses and their trams until electric traction was introduced in April 1901 — the first in London. By 1904 the busy trunk Shepherd's Bush–Uxbridge route had begun, though another depot at Hanwell was to play a larger part in its operation, which ultimately featured the well-known and impressive 'Feltham' cars. Conversion to trolleybuses came in April 1936, but Acton played only a temporary part until work elsewhere could be completed. It closed in March 1937, becoming premises for LT's High Tension Mains Department, which ultimately used it to store electric cables for the Underground. It became a bus garage in 1990, and by early 1995 was allocated 25 Metrobuses and 61 drivers for one-person-operated route 207, the bus route that had replaced the trolleybuses. In 1993, together with a site at Greenford, it replaced the large Hanwell garage.

The centenary of Acton's opening was celebrated in style in 1996 with commemorative badges on all buses based there, and on 20 July RMLs operated special journeys over its former trolleybus routes. Today 30 TNLs — 10.5m Dennis Tridents with Plaxton President bodywork — are based there for the 207. During his tenure as Managing Director of First CentreWest, Peter Hendy described it as 'a solid, cheap-to-run garage with a good future'.

Above:
Two Metrobuses are seen in front of the substantially-built Acton tram depot in early 2000, just before route 207 changed over to low-floor double-deckers. It is probably the oldest London garage in current use. *Author*

Above:
Alperton garage in 1950 is host to a variety of vehicles, including several STLs, two Guy Arabs (one newly repainted) and an RTW, as a fitter attends to the rear blind of an STL. *Geoff Rixon*

ALPERTON (ON)
Corner of Ealing Road and Bridgewater Road, Alperton

Only three Central bus garages were ever built by the LPTB, and today this is the only one to survive. Alperton opened in June 1939 with 58 STLs for 57 scheduled duties. Its opening brought a big reshuffle of routes and vehicles, relieving Cricklewood, Hanwell, Harrow Weald and Willesden garages. During World War 2 the garage undertook body overhauls, this continuing until October 1945.

Being a new garage with high doorways, Alperton was able to take utility Guy Arabs, and at one stage these made up its entire allocation. However, in the early postwar years it also had an allocation of STs for route 187. Ultimately the last Gs were replaced by STLs, which lasted until 1954. A notable allocation was of STL2477, with the experimental body built in 1950 with easy-to-repair prefabricated panels; it was usually known as the 'Meccano set'.

Some RTWs had arrived in 1949 and RTLs in 1950 but both were replaced the following year by RTs.

Although a modern garage, Alperton soon proved inadequate for the area it served. By 1972 about a dozen of the long MB single-deckers parked overnight and all weekend at the Glacier Metals car park just over a canal bridge near the garage, an arrangement that ended only in the summer of 1978. Plans for enlargement were announced in 1973 and started in 1975, but took until June 1978 to finish. LT's Lifts & Escalators Department had to move out to allow its adjacent building to be altered and incorporated into the garage. At the same time, 18 buses (usually the same nine RMs and nine DMSs) were outstationed at Stonebridge.

After the building work was completed an unusual problem appeared. Because the floor level of the former Lifts Department building was higher, the bus washer could only be installed in a part of the garage where the floor sloped, and the mix of soapy water and grease meant buses often slid out of the machine while being washed! Laying a rough, non-slip surface of epoxy resin solved the problem.

The garage had become all-Metrobus by 1982, with both crew and one-person operation. The latter had

Above:
A smart new and, as yet, unblinded Metrobus stands at the doorway of Alperton, the only surviving prewar LPTB Central Area bus garage. *Geoff Rixon*

been introduced at the garage back in 1969, when the RTs on 297 were replaced by MBs, though for the first three months the Merlins did not work on Saturdays.

By 1995 the garage was doing a fair amount of maintenance work and had also become the home for the CentreWest training fleet of 14 BLs. The following year the garage took over operation of route 105 from London & Country together with the low-floor Darts on loan, after that operator had difficulty in working and staffing what was a newly-won tender. A more recent — and permanent — allocation has been of 20 of the final 22 Northern Counties Palatine-bodied Volvo Olympians which were built for stock. Finished to LT specification, they took over route 83, complete with First Challenger fleetnames, and are classed as VNs.

The 2001 allocations saw just two Ms scheduled for work, together with 26 Wright-bodied Dennis Darts, 16 low-floor Dennis Darts with Marshall Capital bodies and a modest nine Dennis Tridents with Plaxton President bodies for route 258.

GREENFORD (G)
Council depot, Greenford Road, Greenford

These premises are leased from the London Borough of Ealing. They were built in the 1930s and are still part of a council depot. They were first used as a midibus base in March 1993, and have an open parking area, offices and a workshop. Use of the premises led to the closure of Hanwell garage. By early 1995 the allocation comprised 110 midibuses and 252 drivers. The whole of the RW

class of Renault midibuses with Wright bodywork was based here: the bodies were well regarded but the chassis were less satisfactory and the complete vehicles were unpopular. A later type not without its problems was the ML class of Marshall Minibuses, all 16 of which were allocated. All soon went. The mid-2001 allocation is rather smaller, but features larger buses, and totals 81 vehicles. There is a mix of eight Leyland Olympians with Alexander or Northern Counties bodies, the remaining vehicles being DMs (44), DMSs (17) and DMLs (12), all these being Marshall Capital-bodied Dennis Dart SLFs with lengths of 9.3m, 8.9m and 10.2m respectively. The depot also housed the articulated Volvo B7LAs and B10LAs that were trialled on the 207 late in 2001.

ST MARY CRAY (Y/OR*)
Faraday Way

A surprising tender win by CentreWest of routes in the Orpington area (a Metrobus stronghold) saw the company's Orpington Buses operation moved to this depot in March 1996 after three months' temporary use of the former London Country garage at Swanley.

A recent development has been the winning of two feeder routes (T31 and T32) to the Tramlink operation at New Addington. Each requires eight Marshall Capital-bodied Dennis Dart SLFs (DMLs). There are 11 shorter versions of the same type (DMS), plus 10 older Dart/Plaxtons (DP), three short Dart/Plaxtons (D) and finally 11 Volvo Olympians with Northern Counties bodywork (V).

UXBRIDGE (UX)

Bakers Road (adjoining the Underground station)

The original Uxbridge garage was a mile or so out of town on the Oxford Road in Denham, being built by the LGOC and opened in 1921. But the following year it passed to Thames Valley, which began running services from Uxbridge on behalf of the LGOC. Single-deckers were used mainly, but there were double-deckers on a route to West Wycombe which passed to Amersham & District in 1930.

The LGOC had taken back the garage from January 1929 to work the routes in the area, and probably put the first of its new Dennis Dart one-man buses into service there in April 1930; they worked the 505 to Richings Park and the 506 to Staines.

At the outbreak of World War 2 the garage was operating ST double-deckers and T and DA single-deckers, though the Darts soon went. After the war it became the last garage to have an all-ST fleet of double-deckers, but in the space of a month in early 1949 all were replaced by RTs.

An extra bay had been added to the garage, but a new garage on another site was a high priority in the late 1940s, though it was not until the 1980s that work began. The new garage came into use in December 1983. It is situated next to the Underground station and occupies the lower ground floor of a new multi-storey building; on the first floor are the traffic offices, a restaurant, a lounge area and an amenities room. On opening it had RMs for route 207, Ms

Above right:
The new Uxbridge garage is situated in the lowest part of a multi-storey building, with the bus station and Underground terminus immediately adjacent. Two different types of Dennis Dart stand outside. *Author*

Right:
A Metrobus stands just outside the newer part of the old Uxbridge garage, with a Bristol LH (in the special Hillingdon livery) and an RM just inside. *Author*

for the 222, 223 and 224, LSs for the 98 and 204 and BLs for the 128. There was room for 65 buses and a staff of over 200.

In 1989 the U-line network was introduced for routes in the area. This was not to do with tendering, but was a marketing initiative by London Buses. The 128 was an early example (for London) of a route with local-authority funding and input. Its BL-class Bristol LHs were modified and fitted with clocks internally, plus an offside indicator designed to show the state of the route and whether the bus going the other way was running late, but there is doubt as to whether the equipment was used very often. The BLs began operating in September 1977 and were later replaced by Leyland Lynxes (LX class).

As well as the busy 207 route to Shepherd's Bush, the garage also operates the 607, a limited-stop version: the same number was once carried by the trolleybuses on the route. Originally LSs and LXs with coach seats were used, but in October 1996 new Volvo Olympians with Northern Counties Palatine II bodywork were introduced, painted in a distinctive livery.

In 1995 the garage was allocated all 14 of London's first type of low-floor single-decker — the LLW-class Dennis Lance SLF with Wright bodywork. By 2001 the schedules at Uxbridge required 10 TNL (10.5m Dennis Trident/Plaxton President) low-floor double-deckers, 13 V-class Olympians (for the 607, mentioned earlier), a few Metrobuses, just one LLW, seven Plaxton- and seven Wright-bodied Dennis Darts and 20 low-floor Dennis Dart SLFs with Marshall Capital bodies.

A final word on the garage comes from First CentreWest's then Managing Director, Peter Hendy: 'Building too complicated, location marvellous'.

WESTBOURNE PARK (X)
Great Western Road, Westbourne Park

By any standards this must be one of the most unusual bus garages, shoe-horned in between the Grand Union Canal and Great Western Road, but with the elevated A40 Westway running literally over the top of part of it. Nearby on the other side is the Hammersmith & City Line of the Underground and the Great Western main line into Paddington.

The London Transport Act of 1972 included powers for acquiring land for building a new garage here, and it duly opened in August 1981, replacing both Middle Row (X) and Stonebridge (SE) garages, but taking the code X (at the insistence of Middle Row staff) instead of the expected WP. The vehicle entrance to the garage is literally beneath the high-level motorway. To one side is a four-storey office block which accommodates operational and engineering staff as well as canteen and recreational facilities. In the entrance to the office block are memorial tablets to the staff of both Middle Row and Stonebridge who lost their lives in World War 2.

When opened, Westbourne Park had an allocation of 78 buses — 47 RM and 31 DM — and an official capacity of 110 vehicles. All operations were initially with crew buses. By 1995 the vehicle allocation totalled 170 buses, but the present figure is even higher: 205.

The space problem has been solved by renting from Railtrack a large open space alongside the railway lines, but potential vandalism problems mean this is not used in the daytime. Because of the huge increase in vehicle numbers the pits provided soon became inadequate. The problem has been neatly solved by adding lifts. Work on double-deckers is undertaken using the pits, while work on the single-deckers takes place in another part of the garage — directly under the motorway, where there is plenty of headroom!

Success with tenders is the main reason for the growth in vehicle numbers. The controversial conversion of two cross-London routes — 28 and 31 — from RM operation (needing 40 buses) to one-person-operation (using 63 Mercedes-Benz 811D midibuses with Alexander bodies with 28 seats and room for 15 standing passengers) also increased the allocation. Since then a third route, the 328, has been introduced, and the three between them now require 69 buses — larger buses, as by 2001 operation of all three was with 9.3m-long low-floor Dennis Dart SLFs with dual-door Marshall bodies seating 22 but with more standing space.

Other Monday–Friday scheduled requirements as at mid-2001 are for 42 RMLs for routes 7 and 23, 47 TNs (10m low-floor Dennis Tridents with Plaxton President bodies) and 20 DMLs (10.2m low-floor Dennis Dart SLFs with dual-door Marshall bodies).

Left:
A five-storey office block fronts Westbourne Park garage, which is built partly under the Westway (M40) viaduct and between the Grand Union Canal and the Great Western main railway line. *Author's collection*

Below:
Routemasters stand under the exit from Westbourne Park garage. Part of the M40 viaduct can be seen above, while one end of the offices is to the left. *Kevin Lane*

LONDON CENTRAL

London Central was bought by Go Ahead Group in September 1994, the purchase being confirmed in October.

BEXLEYHEATH (BX)
Erith Road, Bexleyheath

This was the only new trolleybus depot built by the LPTB — all the others were adaptions of existing tram depots. Power to build was obtained in the London Transport Act (1934) for the first stage of the trolleybus conversion scheme, but the new building was poorly received by the locals; it was in a residential area, and there was a feeling it had been forced through against local wishes.

Liaison between the LPTB's departments was not good in the mid-1930s either, since Traffic Planning staff were enthusiastic about the traffic the new building now being erected was likely to bring, apparently not realising the intended use for the 'factory'.

The depot was described as a large and imposing building and was set back from the road, the depot forecourt being used as a terminus for bus route 122.

Stores and breakdown equipment and a garage for the tower wagon were provided along the north wall of the building, while on the opposite side a two-storey structure had offices, mess room, canteen and billiard room. Behind the depot an open space was used initially to accustom tram drivers to their new vehicles, and then as a turning space for vehicles after they had passed through the washing plant or repair shops. Capacity was described as adequate for 60 trolleybuses, though by 1955 it had a scheduled requirement for 71 vehicles.

Trolleybuses began operating in November 1935 and lasted until March 1959, being replaced by 60 RTs. When the last RTs departed in 1978 the garage became entirely one-person-operated. Some SMs arrived in 1970, but only lasted four years, while the first DMS arrived in 1971, to be followed by the first B20 'quiet' versions in 1977. DMSs monopolised operations for some time until allocation of 60 Ts from 1986; a few Ls arrived subsequently but soon departed.

In August 1986 the garage closed, with work moved to Plumstead, Catford and Sidcup garages. It would not remain closed for long, however, and in January 1988 it reopened as Bexleybus, an autonomous unit within London Buses Ltd — one of a small number set up at

Below:
Bexleyheath was one of the first garages to abandon trolleybuses. Here a 'prewar' RT in use as a trainer is parked on the forecourt with trolleybuses and overhead-line support poles much in evidence. *John Gillham*

about this time, partly to give a better chance of winning tenders against outside bids. The new fleet was quite large. Its double-deckers were a mix of new Northern Counties-bodied Leyland Olympians, which were leased, and two batches of Fleetlines: one batch came from within London Buses, while the others were former London vehicles later used by Clydeside Scottish and now bought back for London. Single-deckers were Leyland Nationals, while small buses were a mix of new MCW Metroriders and RH-class Iveco TurboDailys with Robin Hood bodies previously used at Orpington. All were painted in a new blue and cream livery.

Operations unfortunately got off to a bad start when many drivers from Sidcup depot, which closed, had agreed to move but did not appear. Initially there were grumbles too about limited canteen facilities and lack of a restroom and lockers, while meal reliefs taken away from garage were another cause of complaint. However, operations did improve, and in late 1989 and early 1990 the DMSs were replaced by Titans, but after a few repaints LBL decided buses should be repainted red.

Unfortunately in the next round of tendering Bexleybus retained only one route, the B16, while London Central won nine. The latter had intended to operate from a new base in Crabtree Manor Way, Belvedere, but was refused permission for refuelling facilities. It is said that Selkent, which controlled Bexleybus, was told to include the cost of a new roof for the garage when retendering, whereas the London Central tender bid would not have been based on using the garage anyway. Incidentally, the building had been damaged twice in World War 2 — in 1941 and 1944 — and it could be that repairs then effected were not of high quality.

London Central took over control of the Bexleyheath routes (including the B16) early, from November 1990 instead of from January 1991. The double-deck fleet subsequently became entirely T, with 60 allocated by May 1994, along with 24 MRLs (long Metroriders) and three MTLs (long Reeve Burgess-bodied Mercedes-Benz MB709Ds). By 2001 the fleet allocated was rather bigger, with a scheduled requirement for 139 buses. It included 50 low-floor Volvo B7TL double-deckers with Plaxton bodies (PVLs) for five routes, 32 Volvo Olympian double-deckers with Northern Counties bodies (NVs), and 47 single-deckers. These last comprised 14 Plaxton Pointer 2-bodied Dennis Darts (LDPs) and eight short (DMSs) and 25 long (DMLs) Dennis Darts with Marshall Capital bodies; all three types are low-floor.

CAMBERWELL (Q)
Camberwell New Road, Camberwell Station Road, Camberwell

The original opening date for Camberwell garage was June 1914, but it was used by the War Depaertment from November of that year until July 1919. Once in use it became one of London's biggest garages, and in August 1939 its allocation was of STs and STLs. It carried out body overhauls during 1940 and 1941. Bomb damage in November 1940 destroyed four buses, while 13 others had their bodies damaged beyond repair. For some months afterwards buses were temporarily housed at the old South London Coach Station in Clapham Road which later became a Keith & Boyle vehicle dealership.

Right:
This is the office block of one of London's larger garages, Camberwell, seen as a bus leaves the large covered parking area and turns into Warner Road.
Gerald Mead

Above:
RTLs, an RT and an STL receive attention at the then new dock unit at Camberwell in 1951. *Author's collection*

Below:
A selection of London Central vehicles receive attention in the separate and well-lit dock building in 2000. *Author*

From March 1943 it ran a number of STs towing producer-gas trailers, ultimately operating 16 on route 36; Catford garage also provided some gas buses for the 36. Ultimately Camberwell's total allocation of such buses was 31.

RTLs were the first postwar buses allocated, while a number of SRTs also worked here, along with considerable numbers of standard STLs.

Substantial work was carried out at the garage in the early 1950s. The parking area was extended and the operating and welfare block was reconstructed. At the same time a new dock unit was built at the far end of the area, on the site of property extensively damaged in the war. The large new building was the first in the Central Area to incorporate LT's new ideas on pit and workshop layout. In completely new garages these formed an integral part of the building, but here they were housed in a separate block. The unit was a self-contained workshop with 12 pits — six intended for major work and the others for intermediate docks. Two of the pits contained built-in jacks, and all had exhaust extractors and vacuum-cleaning facilities. The fuel-pump room, smith's shop and battery-charging room were fully enclosed, but the rest of the workshop area was open. An overhead crane and runway served the heavy-docking area, stores and a delivery area. The whole unit was designed to undertake docking for the garage and for the new Walworth garage then under construction across the road — an estimated 350 buses in all.

The RTLs ultimately monopolised the garage's fleet but were replaced by RTs in 1966, the last of these surviving until 1975. A few RMs appeared in 1965, and more followed a few years later. Both DMs and DMSs arrived in 1975, but from 1982 Ts replaced them. Some RMLs joined the RMs in March 1987. Single-deckers were relatively few, with MBs on route 42 from 1970 to 1975 and SMSs on route 188 from 1971 to 1976; a few SMSs later returned to the 42, in 1979/80.

A maximum scheduled requirement of 165 buses in 1952 included 26 operated by staff from New Cross garage, but by 1976 the total was just over 100. Closure of Walworth in 1985 increased the allocation, which totalled 142 in February 1987. In May 1994 it was little changed, at 137, with single-deckers comprising a modest 15 SRs (Mercedes-Benz 811Ds with Optare StarRider bodies). The rest were 37 RMLs, 61 Ts and 24 (ie all but one) of the unique (in London) batch Optare Spectra double-deckers (SPs) dating from 1992/3, which worked on route 3.

Mid-2001 totals were lower, at 114. Of these, 38 were RMLs, 29 were NVs (Northern Counties-bodied Volvo Olympians) and 16 were new AVLs (low-floor Volvo B7TLs with Plaxton President bodies), while single-deckers numbered 24 Dennis Dart SLFs with Plaxton Pointer 2 bodies (LDPs) and seven older Darts with Wright Handybus bodies (DWs). Mention must also be made of three Ts fitted with electronic blinds; two of these acted as standby buses for all Central London Night Buses, irrespective of operator.

NEW CROSS (NX)
New Cross Road

This is said to be London's largest garage, with room for over 300 buses, though it has never housed anywhere near that number; presumably it was considered that the problems of administering such a huge fleet and vast numbers of staff would have been too great. In any event, there were other garages nearby (also former tram depots) that were also not full. But as a result it has been used at times for storage of surplus buses, such as withdrawn 'prewar' RTs; it also stored 15 withdrawn SRT chassis used as a temporary base for new RT bodies that were not required until June 1955, when an overhaul float was established at Aldenham.

New Cross was fully opened by the middle of 1906 and was the LCC's largest tram depot, with space for 280 trams; it had a covered area about 400ft by 400ft, but little street frontage. However, it did have an entrance archway of Portland stone in Roman-Doric style. During World War 2 it carried out overhauls on tramcar bodies, and before the tram-replacement programme began had a maximum requirement for 179 tramcars. Problems with late running or crew changeovers sometimes led to long queues of tramcars outside in New Cross Road.

The depot was involved in three different stages of the tram-replacement scheme, in April 1951, October 1951 (a fairly minor scheme for the depot) and the final stage in July 1952. But the garage was far from ready for any of this, and a host of temporary arrangements were necessary. The April 1951 conversion was partly tied in with the rebuilding of Creek Bridge in Deptford, so buses for this stage were temporarily housed at Peckham (PM), which was not a tram-replacement garage but which had spare space. The final stage introduced three more bus routes, none of which was initially based at New Cross. One went to Camberwell, another to Rye Lane (which was a tram-replacement garage) and a third to Peckham (again). These last three routes were particularly interesting, as they were all worked initially with older buses. 'Prewar' RTs went on the 177 (Abbey Wood–Embankment), and prewar STLs on the 163 (Plumstead Common–Embankment) and 182 (Woolwich–Cannon Street). It was not until late October that New Cross garage started running some buses on its own account, as it were, but by mid-November the garage ran all its allocation from its own premises. Its 53 STLs made it the second-largest STL garage in the fleet, beaten only by Upton Park. But the STLs (eight of which were little newer than the trams they replaced) were only a temporary allocation, and by December newly overhauled RTs were beginning to be allocated.

In July 1966 the garage had a maximum vehicle requirement of 191 buses, including seven RFs for routes 202/202A, and over 10 years later the requirement was still for 182 buses, by which time the fleet was RM, RML and SMS. But by 1987 there had been rather more of a decline, to 124 — a mix of RMs, Ts and Ls (Leyland Olympian / ECW). Between those two periods, from January 1977, the garage had been one of only two to receive new Metropolitans — a type that was to have a relatively short life in London.

The garage has been involved in two activities of particular tourist appeal. In 1972 it was the base for tourist route 100, using the late Prince Marshall's restored ex-Tilling ST on this Central London 'Vintage Bus Service'. More recent was the operation of special Millennium Transit routes M1 and M2 to North Greenwich station for the Dome. The two routes used 17 air-conditioned MD-class East Lancs Myllennium-bodied DAF single-deckers, three of which were LPG-powered. They were intended to use a section of guided busway — to have been the first in London — but it never opened. The buses were double-glazed and of distinctive appearance. They ran on the two services from 1 January 2000 to early in 2001.

Scheduled operations called for 132 buses in mid-2001, comprising 47 RMs/RMLs on busy route 36, 33 NVs (Northern Counties Palatine-bodied Volvo Olympians), 14 Ts and 14 PVLs (9.9m Volvo B7TL low-floor double-deckers with Plaxton President bodywork). The single-deckers included 11 of the striking MDs, plus 10 low-floor LDPs and three step-entrance

DRL-class Dart/Plaxtons. Also based at New Cross was some of the small private-hire fleet, which includes vehicles painted in distinctive original London General-style livery.

PECKHAM (PM)
Copeland Road, Peckham

The new low-cost base here opened in January 1994. It has a capacity for 75 buses and was formerly a local-authority maintenance depot. It is regarded as cheaper to run and well-placed — actually quite near the old garage. It began with some 60 buses: 29 Ts, 14 DRLs (Dennis Dart/Plaxtons), 13 SRs (Mercedes-Benz 811D/ Optare StarRiders) and four MRs (MCW Metroriders).

In January 2000 the garage put into service the first Volvo B7TL low-floor double-deckers (with Alexander bodies) in London, on route 63. The route had a maximum requirement for 24 of these AVLs. Another 16 double-deckers — a mix of Northern Counties- and Alexander-bodied Volvo Olympians (NVs and AVs) — worked on route 381, while two types of Dennis Dart/ Plaxton (DRLs and DPLs) provided 19 buses for the P12 and P13.

Below:
The trams are still at work as building gets underway to convert the vast New Cross depot into a bus garage in May 1952.
John Gillham

LONDON GENERAL

London General was the subject of a management/employee buy-out in November 1994. Some years later it was acquired by Go Ahead Group, which already owned London Central.

BATTERSEA (BB)
Hester Road, Battersea

London General opened a base here in June 1993 as a sub-depot or outstation to Victoria Basement (GB), which was closing. The base was on the site of the annexe to LT's main Battersea garage (B), and was used for midibuses. It was leased from PVS Holdings, a company which specialised in providing parking, servicing and breakdown facilities for operators running to London from mainland Europe and also for smaller operators running coaches into London. PVS Holdings refuelled the buses and cleaned them and also monitored the whole site through closed-circuit television.

Initially some 24 buses, mainly MRLs (Optare MetroRiders), were allocated for routes C1, C3 and 239, but by 1995 the fleet had grown to 42 vehicles — 23 Dennis Darts, 15 Mercedes-Benz 811Ds with Alexander bodies and four Mercedes-Benz 709Ds with Reeve-Burgess bodies featuring tail lifts — for routes C1, 239, 295 and H1: the last-mentioned was operated for the Riverside Health Authority and used the tail-lift-fitted Mercedes. Heavy engineering work on the buses was carried out at Stockwell garage. The 42 buses had a driving staff of nearly 100, and there were two administrative and management staff and three supervisory staff at the base.

The base closed in June 1998, when the routes were reallocated to Putney and Stockwell garages.

MERTON (AL)
High Street and Wandle Bank, Merton

For many years Merton was the LGOC's largest garage, and under the LPTB in 1935 it received an incredible allocation of 222 STLs, eliminating all the NSs and LTs there. But then, a little later, in one of those changes of plan that seem to afflict large organisations, there was a temporary reversion to NSs on one route. By late 1950 it had all 181 utility Daimlers (Ds). Of course, even up to the late 1950s many busy routes had large allocations of buses: for example, in early 1953 the garage was putting out over 50 buses (all Ds) on to route 88, which also had a

Above:
A single London General MetroRider sits among more exotic coaches in the Hester Road, Battersea, base used for a few years in the 1990s. *Author*

Above:
The 1990s extension to Merton garage gave it a wide and unobstructed parking area.
A few Fleetlines are visible among the many Metrobuses. *Author's collection*

small allocation from Hammersmith (R). That same year Merton later received 126 new buses, bringing its RT fleet to 132 at the end of the year.

The garage had been built by the LGOC in 1913, and opened in the November. By the outbreak of World War 2 it was still running its STL fleet, plus some Q single-deckers. It carried out body overhauls during 1940/1. In May 1944 the garage was allocated the first low-height utility Ds, for route 127, ultimately receiving all 10 of the type, delivered in two batches; they replaced lowbridge STs and STLs that were urgently needed to augment the low-height fleet at other garages.

Up to 1950 the utility D allocation had totalled 139, plus a fair number of STLs. When new RTs replaced the utility fleet of 42 Ds on Green Line work at Romford there was a dispute over the displaced buses, as the union felt they should move elsewhere in the Country Area, but the Country Bus & Coach Department did not want a different type introduced to its other garages, with attendant training difficulties. The staff at Merton were concerned about the deterioration of some of their STLs and asked for the Ds, not knowing about the

union's refusal to accept them for 'red bus' work. Initially these green Ds went into service still in green livery, with just the fleetnames changed. The fleet of utility Ds, even without the green-liveried additions, gave the garage the greatest allocation of utility buses in the UK.

The last D ran in early January 1953. Earlier the garage had also had three postwar Daimler CVG6s with Brush bodies on hire from Maidstone Corporation; they were used for about 18 months in 1949/50. In 1952 low-bridge RLHs replaced the low-height Ds on the 127; the RLHs went when the route was withdrawn in 1958. The garage had RFs for route 200, but these moved away when the route was double-decked in 1965.

A garage modernisation scheme was completed in 1960. But the garage was long and narrow and another modernisation and rebuilding scheme was completed relatively recently — in September 1991, after two years' work which included fitting a new roof and a new sprinkler system, demolition of the old stores area and removal of the old inspection pits. New washrooms with showers were provided, and the internal rearrangement gave an unobstructed area of constant width for parking. During rebuilding, some buses were parked in a yard at nearby Collier's Wood.

Introduction of flat-fare route M1 in 1969 had brought MBSs to the garage, with MBs and RMs arriving in 1970, DMSs and SMSs in 1971 and LSs in 1982. MBs and MBSs went in 1974 and SMSs in 1977, with crew operation finishing in February 1987 with the removal of the RMs.

Over the years the total number of buses has declined considerably. In May 1952 the maximum requirement was for 195 buses. By November 1976 it was down to 134, while the February 1987 total was just 83. It subsequently improved, and by May 1994 was up to 116, of which the double-deck complement was 77 Ms, with Dennis Darts and Optare MetroRiders making up the total. By mid-2001 the fleet was more standardised with 67 PVLs (low-floor Volvo B7TLs with Plaxton President bodies), just three Ms and 49 LDPs (low-floor Dennis Dart SLFs with Plaxton Pointer 2 bodies).

PUTNEY (AF)
Chelverton Road, Putney

Situated in an otherwise residential road just off Putney's busy and congested high street, this garage has an ancestry going back to horse-bus days. First used as horse-bus stables in 1888, it became a motor-bus garage in 1912. Much rebuilding and modernisation was carried out in 1935/6, and further improvements were made in 1985/6. But the road still seems an unlikely setting for a bus garage, the size of which is by no means obvious from its modest frontage. During the mid-1930s rebuilding, buses on route 30 were temporarily housed at the former Chiswick tram depot. Then the 30 was worked by LT double-deckers, but

Above:
On a sunny summer's day, bus crew sit on benches outside the surprisingly small frontage of Putney (Chelverton Road) garage, seen before modernisation. *John Gillham*

Below:
In 1947 two hired Bedford OB coaches mix with 'prewar' RTs, an LTC and a 'Bluebird' ST or LT trainer in Chelverton Road garage. *Author's collection*

after it returned home STLs were allocated. Only three years earlier the allocation had consisted of most of the remaining NS-type double-deckers with solid tyres and covered tops: roof clearance was too tight for covered-top NSs with pneumatic tyres.

The garage became well known in being the first to put into service the so-called 'prewar' RTs, from January 1940. These displaced STLs but were initially plagued with brake problems, and many were with-drawn and stored until modifications could be made; STs temporarily replaced them. For much of the war the garage was under-utilised operationally and was used to store quantities of delicensed buses.

The garage was known as Chelverton Road until 1963, when it was officially renamed Putney, belated recognising the closure a few years previously of Putney Bridge garage.

The last 'prewar' RTs went in 1955, being briefly replaced by postwar RTs, which within months had themselves been replaced by RTLs. RTWs had been allocated from 1952 and lasted until 1965. RMs arrived in late 1962 and RMLs four years later; the latter are still there today, with a scheduled requirement of 38 for routes 14 and 22. Other types have come and gone, with SMSs for route 85 in 1971 being replaced by DMSs about a year later; more DMSs appeared later. The DMSs were replaced in 1983 by Ms, a few of which are still allocated to the garage in 2001.

The busy route 74 has a requirement in 2001 for 24 Volvo Olympians with Northern Counties Palatine II bodies. These are route-branded, though in such a way that they can operate on Sundays and late evenings on route 14; when they entered service, their drivers were issued with 'Route 74' ties and badges and also a booklet giving answers to the most common questions posed by would-be passengers.

Other mid-2001 scheduled requirements call for 34 Dennis Dart / Plaxton Pointer single-deckers, plus four of the more recent low-floor version. The other low-floor buses at the garage are just four Volvo B7TL/ Plaxton Presidents for Putney's small share of work on route 37.

STOCKWELL (SW)
Lansdowne Way and Binfield Road, Stockwell

Without doubt, Stockwell is London's best-known garage, and it also has the rare distinction (for a bus garage) of being a listed building. Yet at the beginning there had been no intention of creating an architectural masterpiece. It was only in the middle of 1948, when detailed planning for replacing the remaining trams with buses was underway, that it was realised that the new Stockwell bus garage was a vital part of the scheme and that, for it to be finished by early 1951, work would have to start in late 1948. But detailed design was not even completed by early 1949, and mid-1951 was by then the earliest possible completion date; luckily temporary parking space could be arranged.

At that time almost all building materials were in short supply, and the architecturally striking design, featuring a reinforced concrete barrel roof, was chosen to over-come shortages of the steel which would otherwise have been needed with more conventional construction. But materials for the roof were delayed anyway, and con-struction did not start when planned because of the need to demolish some houses on the site; they could not be knocked down until their inhabitants were rehoused, and it took time to find new homes for them.

The main building is nearly 400ft long and is con-structed of reinforced concrete arched ribs spanning

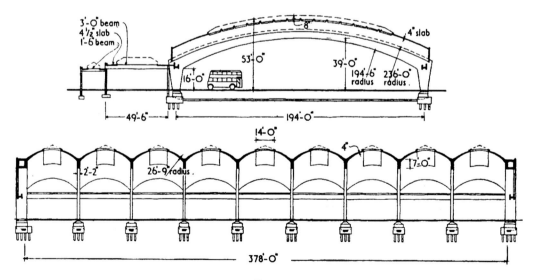

Above:
Cross-section (top) and longitudinal section (below) of the unique Stockwell garage.
Author's collection

Top:
The dramatic roofline and unobstructed parking space are clearly visible. Also just distinguishable among the vehicles are two of LT's mobile canteens and one of Western SMT's Guy Arab coaches. *Author*

Above:
A view through the exit doorway in the early days (before the garage was completed) shows part of the roof and some of the RTLs allocated. *Author*

194ft, connected by arch vaults spanning 42ft, to give nine bays and an uninterrupted floorspace of 73,350sq ft. The traffic offices are in a separate building, while the docking and repair section is an annexe at one corner of the main building but outside it. A 40hp installation for vacuum cleaning allows eight operators in the main cleaning and refuelling area to work simultaneously and enables both decks of a bus to be cleaned out at the same time in each of the four servicing areas.

It was early April 1952 when the garage opened for business, instead of the originally planned date of October 1950. For its first four days it ran just 11 buses on the 178 which had moved in from their temporary home at Rye Lane, but a few days later it gained more tram-replacement work from the next stage of that scheme, so that it now had 38 RTLs, all acquired secondhand in transfers from other garages that had received new RTs in replacement. The garage was not finally completed until autumn 1953. However, after the RTLs arrived in 1952 it received some STLs for operating the summer-only Festival Gardens route B.

Elsewhere in London the staff recruitment problem was beginning to get difficult, so in November 1953 route 77 was moved to Stockwell from Gillingham Street, Victoria, together with 13 postwar STDs. In March the following year more work arrived from the same garage when route 77A was also transferred. This increased the scheduled peak requirement to 110 buses, following the closure of Nunhead garage earlier in the same year. By 1966 the total had increased again, to 126 buses, including RMs and RMLs which had joined the RTLs.

From the 1970s the garage provided vehicles for the Round London Sightseeing Tour, including Obsolete Fleet's ex-Midland Red D9s converted to open-top, ex-Bournemouth Corporation DMO Fleetlines with removable roofs and, for a time, FRM1. For the same service, from 1973 to 1978 the garage was also allocated new DMs and DMSs, which worked for just six months before being transferred away; this met the Bus Grant requirement that vehicles work at least half their mileage in the first year on stage work.

In summer 1979 the garage worked the not very successful Shoplinker service between Oxford Street and Knightsbridge with 16 RMs in a dedicated red and yellow livery. Then in 1984 it was chosen for comparative testing of new vehicles on route 170 (Aldwych–Roehampton). The route was chosen because it was worked by only one garage, and the garage was chosen because it had had no experience of Ms or Ts in its fleet to prejudice it. This trial fleet consisted of two or three each of Leyland Olympians, Mk 2 Metrobuses, Dennis Dominators and Volvo Ailsas, of which the most interesting was the twin-stair Ailsa, V3.

In 1993 Stockwell was allocated the small fleet of 12m-long single-deck VNs — Volvo B10Bs with Northern Counties bodies — for route 88, marketed as The Clapham Omnibus. Unfortunately parked cars, particularly in the evenings, made operation of such long buses difficult, and they were eventually replaced by Ms. However, they were still working on the 88 in

May 1994 when the allocation also included 67 Ms and 35 VCs (underfloor-engined Volvo Citybuses with Northern Counties bodywork), plus 17 9m Dennis Darts and nine MRLs — a grand total of 139 buses. In mid-2001 totals were lower, but there was a much larger number of recent vehicles, including 64 low-floor double-deckers for four routes: most were PVLs (Volvo B7TLs with Plaxton President bodies) but there were also 13 PDLs (Dennis Tridents with similar bodies), the latter usually on route 88. The rest of the total was made up by 32 VCs and just seven single-deckers — low-floor Dennis Dart SLFs with Plaxton Pointer bodies of the LDP class.

SUTTON (A)
Bushey Road, Sutton

The LGOC opened Sutton garage in January 1924 on what was then described as a fine corner site. It cost £30,000 to build, had an area of 37,000sq ft, and its equipment included petrol tanks of 13,000gal capacity and a washing machine. It had a capacity of 100 buses but by 1926 only about 40 were allocated there. However, the opening of the Northern Line Underground extension to Morden the same year and later a new Southern Electric branch line sparked off rapid development of the area, with considerable house-building. Five new routes were introduced from the garage as feeders to the Underground, and these were originally worked by K-type single-deckers in a distinctive silver-grey livery.

By mid-1939 the allocation consisted of STLs and LT single-deckers. There had been an earlier brief interlude when the Dennis Lance fleet of double-deckers at Potters Bar was moved to Sutton, at the end of 1936, but they were then all withdrawn between November and December 1937, though less than six years old.

In 1946 the STLs were moved out when the fleet of 100 Park Royal-bodied Daimler double-deckers were moved in; scheduled operation required 95 double-deckers. The last D ran in January 1953 — RTLs started to replace them in 1952.

Single-deck LTs were based at the garage for years, those for route 213 being replaced by RFs. However, in 1941 the LTs on the 245 were replaced by lowbridge double-deckers on loan from Manchester Corporation and Hants & Dorset and then by lowbridge STs from Watford in the Country Area, the route being renumbered 127. Soon afterwards it was transferred to Merton garage. The RFs on the 213 lasted until it was double-decked in 1963, and in 1972 DMSs were allocated.

The RTLs had been replaced by RTs in 1953/4, remaining on all double-deck routes until conversion to one-person-operated DMSs in the early 1970s. The last RTs were replaced by RMs on route 93 in 1976, in turn being replaced by DMSs in 1982. But since 1969 routes 80/80A had been worked by RFs, which were replaced by BLs in 1976. These routes were recast and reverted to double-deck in 1981 and from September 1982 the whole fleet comprised the DMS type.

Above:
The tree-lined street along the side of Sutton garage plays host to three Fleetlines — two based at the garage and the other, plus a Metrobus, from Norbiton. *Author*

In May 1952 the total scheduled requirement had been for 128, this falling to 100 by mid-1966, to 82 by late 1976 and to 62 by February 1987. By May 1994 it had increased to 85, including some 75 Ms which had replaced the DMSs, plus four Dennis Darts and six Optare MetroRiders. Mid-2001 saw an allocation of 82 buses for LT tendered work, plus about 10 buses for various Surrey County Council services, private school contracts, Tesco contracts and a Kingston University contract. In summer one bus, usually an open-topper, was provided for the London by Night tour which London General runs from Central London. Buses on LT work were 56 NVs (Volvo Olympians with Northern Counties bodies) and 26 low-floor Dennis Darts with Plaxton bodies.

The garage was one of the last to receive substantial improvements before privatisation, the work including reroofing, moving the maintenance section, demolishing an old air-raid shelter and providing extra covered accommodation at the rear of the garage, near allotments.

An unusual operation begun in 1989 after Cityrama withdrew from route 200 was its working by Suttonbus from a small yard near the Merton Abbey Savacentre. Drivers were drawn from Sutton garage, but maintenance was subcontracted to Merton. Buses carried an AA code.

WATERLOO (Red Arrow) (RA)
Cornwall Road, Waterloo

This opened as the Cornwall Road bus stand in time for the Festival of Britain in 1951 for services terminating at Waterloo. For many years it was a simple bus stand (not station) for buses to lay over but also had a canteen and staff facilities.

In the 1980s a scheme was devised to establish a permanent base for the Red Arrow buses at Cornwall Road, moving them from Victoria and Ash Grove garages. The cost was estimated at £245,000, but there were problems with planning permission, and the Red Arrows were temporarily housed at Walworth garage.

Planning permission was eventually granted by the Secretary of State for Transport in February 1989, and the scheme was re-costed at £830,000. Later that year the London Buses board gave approval for the work to go ahead. It involved providing fuelling facilities, washing equipment, offices for supervisory staff and for cash handling and various measures to keep down the level of noise and reduce pollution. All 42 Red Arrow LSs — recoded GLS after they were rebuilt by East Lancs as National Greenways — were allocated there.

The closure of Victoria garage later resulted in the

RMLs for route 11 being transferred there. Like the Red Arrow routes they only ran on Mondays to Fridays, with Stockwell garage providing one-person-operated double-deckers for the 11 at weekends.

However, the depot has continued to attract complaints from local residents — the site is bordered by housing on two sides. In mid-2001 it was announced that London General had won tenders for the operation of three-door 18m-long articulated buses on the Red Arrow routes from spring 2002, leading to suggestions that the Waterloo site might revert to a bus terminal, with the buses (including RMLs) being moved to Stockwell.

Top:
Until relatively recently, Cornwall Road, Waterloo, was a bus stand with facilities for crews. Metrobuses, an Olympian and two Red Arrow National 2s (based at Ash Grove) are visible in this 1987 view. *Author*

Above:
In 1990 the bus stand became a depot for all the Red Arrow routes and subsequently also for Routemasters used on route 11 on Mondays to Fridays. *Kevin Lane*

London United was the subject of a management/employee buy-out in November 1994. It later acquired Stanwell Buses (trading as Westlink), which had been the first London bus company to be sold to its management, in January 1994 — several months in advance of other bus companies; West Midlands Travel took control of the company a few months later but then sold it the following year to London United.

In 1998 London United was bought by French company Transdev.

FULWELL (FW)
Wellington Road and Stanley Road, Fulwell

This had been the main depot of the London United Tramways, built on an 11-acre site in 1902. When new it was described as one of the finest plants of its kind in the country, 'in every way admirably appointed'. The LUT actually intended it to be the centre of a vastly greater tramway network than ever materialised. Its solid and imposing structure has stood the test of time well, and it is now unusual among London bus garages in being divided into two. On one side is the London United garage, while to the rear is a separate section (once used by London Bus Sales) for the buses of Tellings-Golden Miller.

London's first trolleybuses began running in May 1931 and were based here; of these, trolleybus No 1 is now owned by the London Transport Museum. The depot building was reconstructed in 1937 after the LPTB acquired the freehold. Fifty years later the workshops, staff accommodation and offices were refurbished and the garage was rerroofed. Officially, trolleybus capacity was for 120 vehicles, with some 90 scheduled in 1950. Though the first trolleybuses had begun running in 1931, it was not until October 1935 that the last tram route at the depot was converted. As well as operating its own allocation of trolleybuses, Fulwell depot also received all new examples on delivery to check them over before they entered service at various garages. It also carried out overhauls.

Together with Isleworth, Fulwell was one of the last two depots to run trolleybuses, on 8 May 1962. As with most other stages of the trolleybus conversion scheme, not all routes were directly replaced, and a number of existing bus services and garages were also involved. Some of Fulwell's trolleybus-replacement work went to Norbiton garage, which in turn moved other routes to Kingston and Merton garages, while Fulwell became the first ex-trolleybus depot to gain a single-decker route, the 206, then worked with RFs.

RMs and the RFs were the only buses at the garage until Twickenham garage closed in 1970, bringing RTs and SMs. The RTs went early in 1972, having been partly replaced by DMSs from 1971, and from March 1979 the first production Metrobuses began to oust the DMSs. Further single-deckers, in the shape of SMSs, came in March 1971, and the garage was the first to get SMSs converted to SMDs (with centre exits sealed and

Above:
Within a month London's last trolleybuses will have gone and the former London United Tramways Fulwell depot will have become a bus garage. Tram track disused for more than 25 years still remains in the cobbled road surface. *John Gillham*

Above:
Routemasters and RFs are now standard fare, while three RTW training buses can also be seen in this 1967 view. But the tram track still survives. *Author*

Below:
Volvo double-deckers and Dennis Dart single-deckers were the order of the day by 1999. But intruders, relatively speaking, were some Arriva-liveried and -operated DAFs for route 85 (based on the forecourt and not in the garage) and a preserved Royal Blue coach, the latter having brought members of the Omnibus Society on a visit. *Stephen Morris*

extra seats added), in 1976; BLs also arrived the same year. Departing that year were the RFs, SMs, and SMSs. The SMDs were succeeded by LSs in 1978, but these lasted only until 1980. When the BLs left in spring 1982 the garage became all-double-deck and from 1985 entirely one-person-operated.

The total number of buses at the depot had varied: to be precise, from 84 trolleybuses in 1955 to 59 buses in 1966, then up to 87 by 1976 and down to 82 in 1987. But by 1984 numbers were up considerably, to 101, with 40 Ms, 36 DTs (Dennis Darts with Carlyle or Duple Dartline bodies) and 25 DRs (Darts with Reeve-Burgess or Plaxton Pointer bodies). The mid-2001 total had again edged up, to 107. Ms, at 24, no longer formed the largest class, as there were 31 VAs (Volvo Olympians with Alexander RH bodies), along with 17 DPSs (Dennis Dart SLFs with Plaxton Pointer 2 bodies), 16 DRs and 8 DRLs (Reeve-Burgess or Plaxton-bodied Dennis Darts of 8.5m or 9m length). Finally there were 11 DNs — DAF double-deckers with Northern Counties Palatine II bodies. These were bought new by Arriva Croydon & North Surrey; after its Leatherhead garage closed suddenly at the end of April 1999, Arriva continued to operate these on route 85 (Kingston–Putney) from the forecourt of Fulwell garage, using Arriva drivers. Then in September 1999 operation of the route and 12 of the 13 buses used on it were transferred to London United.

HEATHROW WEST RAMP (WR)

In January 1995 the Ms on routes A1 and A2 from Heathrow to Central London that had been allocated to Stamford Brook were reallocated here, though maintenance work was still undertaken at their former base. By the summer, the West Ramp fleet had been boosted by 16 DT-class Duple-bodied Dennis Darts which had been refitted with luggage racks, coach seats and air conditioning for use on Airbus Direct, a new service between the airport and major London hotels. It did not prove successful.

The Metrobuses for the A1 and A2 were replaced by 19 new air-conditioned Volvo Olympians with Alexander Royale bodywork, delivered in two batches in 1995/6. But the service (by then just one route, the A2) and vehicles were sold to National Express (AirLinks) early in 2000, and London United then ceased to use the base.

HOUNSLOW (AV)
Kingsley Road, Hounslow

The LGOC opened Hounslow garage in December 1913, building it on the site of the former Hounslow Town branch of the District Railway that had closed in 1909. The garage was requisitioned in January 1915 and

Above:
Neat and clean brickwork characterises the rebuilt Hounslow garage in the 1950s as an RT leaves with its conductor upstairs resetting the destination blinds. *Author*

Above:
Hounslow garage in 1984 sees a line of Leyland Nationals, plus two of the former British Airways Routemasters in use as staff buses. *Kevin Lane*

did not reopen for bus operations until July 1919. In 1925 it was allocated the first pneumatic-tyred single-deck K types, which were used first on new Staines–Slough route 162A, which extended on Saturday afternoons and Sundays to Burnham Beeches as route 162. Another first for the garage came in April 1930, when it gained the first two of a new small-bus fleet — the original Dennis Dart (type DA). They were 7ft 2in-wide one-man buses with 18 seats. However, traffic of a more local nature needed rather larger buses, and soon afterwards the garage roof was raised to allow closed-top double-deckers to enter.

Before the outbreak of war the garage was running STs, DAs and some T (AEC Regal) single-deckers; the last-mentioned were apparently for the use of Uxbridge garage. In 1946 Hounslow's only double-deckers were STs, with a fleet of 66 plus spares, while six single-deck LTs were required for route 237. But the numbers escalated over the next few years. An LT survey of garages and garage space in 1947 found 92 buses allocated, of which only 72 could be housed in the garage; luckily there was spare land behind on which to park the others. A further problem was that buses terminating at Hounslow garage all had to find space inside while on layover. Even at this stage it was realised that plans to develop Heathrow as London's airport were likely to increase demand.

The garage was rebuilt and extended, covering the site of the existing one, plus extra space including the old arches of the District Railway viaduct, which were demolished. The problem with the terminating buses was solved by using additional land (already owned) to build a bus station fronting on to London Road, so that incoming buses could either terminate there or run straight into the garage. The administrative block was built between the bus station and London Road, rather than adjacent to the garage itself. By the time the building was completed in 1954 the garage's scheduled requirement had gone up again, to 100, with a total allocation of 112 buses. Later it was to fall to 85, but managed to top 100 again in May 1962 when it took on the replacement buses after Isleworth trolleybus depot (just along the London Road) closed.

Hounslow's first postwar buses were RTs, allocated in the latter half of 1948 at a time when the garage was still operating one or two open-staircase ex-Tilling STs, and it later gained some STLs. RMs appeared initially as trolleybus replacements, but it was not until 1978 that RMLs arrived. From 1969 onwards, MBs, SMs and SMSs appeared, a notable vehicle being SMS838, the last AEC Swift — indeed, the last new AEC of any kind — bought by LT. Upon their arrival in March 1972, this bus and a few others replaced Hounslow's last RTs.

Four years later the garage received a big batch of LSs — 51 in all — which were a cancelled order for Venezuela; although they had doors and driving position on the correct side, they were not to LT specification and were intended as a stopgap to replace SMSs. They were joined by the six original LSs from Dalston garage. Smaller single-deckers, in the shape of RFs, had worked route 237 since December 1952 when they had replaced LT single-deckers, and survived at the garage until 1977 (by then working another route as well), when BLs took over — for about a year.

The last of the AEC Merlins (MBSs) had gone in September 1972 when they had been replaced by SMSs with additional luggage space for use on route A1 to Heathrow; operations to the airport became a significant part of the garage's workload, particularly before the Underground's Piccadilly Line was extended.

The garage had also been the first in London to operate a low-floor single-decker when it received Dennis Lance SLF / Wright Pathfinder LLW1 after exhibition

at Bus & Coach '93 at the National Exhibition Centre in Birmingham in October. This bus and its sisters went into service on route 120 but have since moved on, the route being worked in 2001 by Volvo B7TL double-deckers with either Alexander ALX400 (VA class) or Plaxton President (VP) bodywork. These low-floor double-deckers are also intermixed on two other routes (337 and H32), while the Alexander-bodied version alone is additionally used on route 220. Adding further variety are three low-floor Dennis Trident/Alexanders. A handful of Leyland-bodied Leyland Olympians plus a few Metrobuses make up the rest of the double-deck fleet, while single-deckers comprise 63 low-floor Dennis Dart/Plaxton Pointer 2s plus a few step-entrance Darts. The grand total of 127 scheduled buses takes the garage above the planned capacity of 120 of 45 years ago, when buses were smaller anyway.

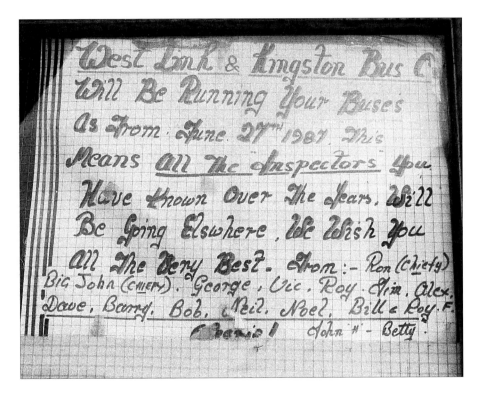

The first moves to establish Westlink (here wrongly spelt) as a company within LT came in 1987. *Author*

HOUNSLOW HEATH (WK/HH)
Pulborough Way, Green Lane, Hounslow

This was the base used by Westlink under the code WK when it began operations. Following the company's acquisition by London United, the code was changed to HH in 1999. Stanwell Buses, trading as Westlink, began with three London contracts in conjunction with Surrey County Council. These were the 116 (Hounslow–Staines–Thorpe Park), 117 (Brentford–Ashford Hospital/Staines) and 203 (Brentford–Staines). A fleet of 28 Leyland Nationals (LSs) was used.

London United subsequently took out a 20-year lease on the former Travellers Coach base at Tamian Way, Hounslow, which is adjacent to the ex-Westlink depot. Among the vehicles based here is the CD class of eight Wright Crusader-bodied Dennis Dart SLFs, a type rare in London; they work route H25.

Above:
Kingston Bus Station must have been one of the most photographed locations; this view, taken on Christmas Day 1978, when no buses ran from the garage, shows Bristol LHs and RFs parked there. *Geoff Rixon*

KINGSTON (K)
Richmond Road and Cromwell Road, Kingston

Kingston was a modest-sized garage when it was opened by the LGOC in January 1922, and served 'exclusively rural traffic requirements'. Thirty years later, Driver Fennemore reminisced on its early days that 'there was time . . . to stop and set a rabbit trap on the Guildford route and collect your prize on the return journey'. Longer routes such as that passed to the LPTB's Country Bus & Coach Department in the 1930s; in the meantime a small outstation at Weybridge (code WB) had opened in May 1923, and this survived until December 1939.

The area around Kingston developed rapidly, while the town itself became a busy suburban shopping centre. A bus station was opened in front of the garage in 1928, and this in due course eased the overnight parking problems as the allocation grew. But by 1947, out of a total allocation of 90 buses, 17 were being parked overnight on the forecourt of the nearby railway station (where there was also a small, primitive bus station) and a further 21 in a municipal car park.

When the new garage at nearby Norbiton opened in May 1952, Kingston's allocation dropped from 87 to 47 buses, which could all (just) be kept under cover, though a former coal yard opposite the garage was to see further use as a bus park. Norbiton was finally extended in 1984, and Kingston then closed, though buses still had to drive through it to reach the bus station. Closure

lasted only from January 1984 to June 1987, when Kingston reopened as a maintenance base for the 22 MCW Metroriders in the new 'Kingston Hoppa' fleet operated by Stanwell Buses, then a new subsidiary of London Buses; overnight they parked in a car park in Cromwell Road. In 1990 Stanwell Buses (using the Westlink fleetname) won a tender for the 131, and from September a fleet of Ts (Titans) formerly at Camberwell was allocated to Kingston.

After many false rumours the bus station finally closed (but not the garage); the town is unusual in having two modern bus stations, one of them almost opposite the garage site and covering the former coal yard once used for parking. By mid-1994 Westlink had a maximum requirement for 55 buses, the fleet including Metroriders, Titans and Darts. The parking problems were back, with, for example, 20 vehicles being outstationed overnight at the Kingston Business Centre in 1997; by this time Westlink was owned by London United. The problem worsened in 2000 when the whole bus station and garage was demolished for redevelopment, with yet more temporary parking spaces being used pending the hoped-for opening of new premises at Tolworth in 2001.

At various times when Kingston was under pressure, LT tried unsuccessfully to buy the cinema that occupied the corner site next to the bus station and garage. Ironically the new development going up in 2001 includes a multiplex cinema.

Over the years the garage has had more than its fair

Above:
The garage and its servicing facilities were cramped and handicapped by the need for buses in service to drive through to reach the bus station. Here two RFs and an LH stand by the pit area. *Geoff Rixon*

share of uncommon types. It was also unusual in that some of its crews and their single-deckers worked on more than one route in a day, for example routes 201/213 and 215/218/219. Until early 1938 the garage or outstation were home for the three experimental Chiswick-built single-deckers, T1000-2. It was the first garage to receive the new rear-engined Leyland Cubs of the CR class in September 1939; they were withdrawn in 1942 because of spares shortages, and further bonneted C-class Leyland Cubs were allocated. At the end of August 1939 the allocation had been of five different types: ST, single-deck LT, T, Q and DA (Dennis Dart).

At various dates between October 1944 and April 1946, three experimental pay-as-you-board double-deckers with seated conductors were tried on route 65; all were modified standard buses. In order of arrival they were STL1793, STL2284 and RT97.

In the early postwar years the fleet was very mixed and included ex-Tilling and ex-LGOC T-type AEC Regals, ex-Green Line petrol-engined Ts and 1946-built postwar Ts, plus single-deck LTs. Soon TDs were added, and the ex-Tilling and ex-Green Line Ts went, but former Country Area Q types also arrived. The ex-LGOC T-type buses gained diesel engines in 1949 and 1950 and were the only buses light enough to be allowed over Walton Bridge; they lasted until 31 January 1953 and were replaced by ex-Green Line 10T10s dating from 1938, a new 'temporary' bridge having by then been opened.

Eventually Kingston became well-known for its RFs — London's last — which finished at the end of March

1979; 15 of them worked on the final day, and there were farewell tours next day. BLs had already taken over much RF work, but service cuts meant the 218 and 219 now required the larger LS; when on Kingston's pits this type would have obstructed the entrance from the garage to the bus station, so the routes had to move to Norbiton, with other operations passing to Kingston in exchange. In September 1982 more routes were converted from BL to LS (to cope with service cuts), so BL operation ended at Kingston, and all of route 65 and its RMs came back in return.

SHEPHERDS BUSH (S)
Wells Road, Shepherds Bush

The original garage in Wells Road was built by the London Motor Omnibus Company (better known by its 'Vanguard' fleetname) in 1906 but opened in February 1907 and came under LGOC control after the amalgamation of 1908. The premises were requisitioned by the War Department in World War 1 but reopened in 1919 (albeit not fully operational). They closed again in January 1920 for 'rebuilding' and reopened in July 1923. However, the new building was still somewhat cramped and had space for only about 50 buses.

In the early 1950s a new garage was built in a complicated fashion over and around the existing one, as this had to continue in use. Some of the extra land used had been the site of the railway line from Olympia

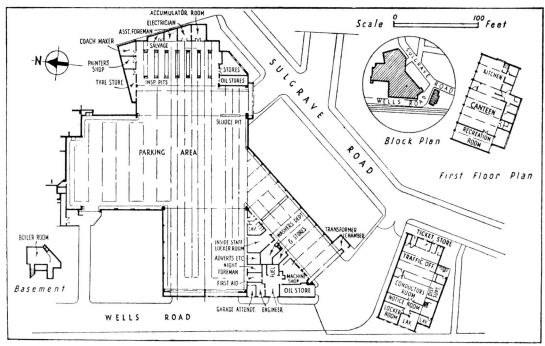

A layout plan for Shepherds Bush garage shows the very irregular layout of the site.
Modern Transport

Above:
Beams and crossbeams delineate the roof of Shepherds Bush garage while RTLs park below.
The dock area is visible in the distance. *Author*

Top left:
Withdrawn postwar STDs fill a spare corner of the garage in 1955. *Author*

Below:
A Metrobus (on a former trolleybus service) and a Fleetline trainer arrive at the garage
while a Routemaster parks within in this 1984 view. *Kevin Lane*

to Ravenscourt Park, which had been disused for very many years. Provision for parking was made on the extended site, and alternative office and canteen accommodation had to be provided.

A notable feature of the new garage is the support for the roof by reinforced concrete bowstring girders which carry a system of hollow box girders. There are three bowstring spans, of differing lengths, which rise above the general roof level, and each rests at either end on roller bearings. The very irregular shape of the completed garage is shown by the drawing on page 120. The unusual form of construction (for the time) was dictated by steel shortages, but the building work was then held up by a shortage of timber needed for the shuttering, then by a shortage of cement and finally by a lack of reinforcing rods. The garage had room for 123 buses, but if required could be extended to accommodate another 25. Unfortunately its allocation has never reached even 100 buses.

Before World War 2 the complete allocation comprised double-deck LTs, ultimately replaced by RTLs and then RTWs too. In October 1957 the BEA airport coaches moved here from Victoria, displacing some stored and (so far) unused RTLs to Clapham garage. Then, in July 1960, the airport coaches were moved again, to the former Hammersmith trolleybus depot (HB), while the replacement RMs for the Hammersmith-based trolleybus routes and their crews came to Shepherd's Bush. Some 57 RMs were allocated for this work.

By the mid-1960s the fleet was a mix of RTs and RMs, with a total scheduled requirement of 71 buses. In January 1971 the garage became one of the first two (the other being Brixton) to operate one-person DMSs, on former trolleybus route 220. By 1983 Ms had displaced the DMSs, but RMLs (allocated from 1975)

and RMs were still active in 1987. Just two types were operated by May 1994: RMLs (38) and Ms (18). The 2001 total was higher, with 38 RMLs for the 9 and 94, 18 low-floor double-deckers in the shape of Alexander-bodied Volvo B7TLs (VA class) and 32 low-floor Dart/Plaxton single-deckers of various configurations.

STAMFORD BROOK (V)
Chiswick High Road

The premises here have had a chequered career despite their long life, often being used for storage purposes. Known for many years as Chiswick Tram Depot — even well after trams had vanished from the entire area — it was originally horse-tram stables which began operating in 1883. It was replaced by a new depot on the same site which opened in July 1901. Flags and bunting adorned it as the venue for an impressive banquet marking the inauguration of London's first public electric tramway. Also included on the site was a generating station of considerable architectural merit, which ultimately became subject to a preservation order.

However, London United Tramways' vast new depot at Fulwell soon put Chiswick in the shade, and it was bought by the LCC in 1917 together with the LUT's Hammersmith tram lines. The LCC kept a number of cars here from 1922 to 1932 but never made great use of the depot.

Part of the building was used for buses from July 1935 to March 1936 while Chelverton Road (Putney) bus garage was being rebuilt. LTs were allocated here and used on route 30, under the code letters CK, being still operated by Putney crews. Later in the 1930s, redundant Dennis Lance double-deckers were stored here for a time. The premises were also used for quite substantial rebuilding of some of the early standard trolleybuses, but these early examples were still the first to go when the trolleybus-replacement scheme got underway in the late 1950s.

The depot carried out body overhauls during the war and in the early postwar period and later became one of the locations reconditioning STLs to be used in the last stage of the tram-replacement scheme. In 1966 the BEA fleet was moved in from the former Hammersmith (HB) trolley-bus depot, staying until August 1978 when the (by now smaller) fleet moved again, to Stonebridge garage. Another minor job done at the garage was the signwriting on the silver-painted Silver Jubilee RMs following their overhaul at Aldenham.

Above:
An STL, a Green Line Q and a single-deck LT are all in for bodywork attention at the former Chiswick tram depot in 1951, when it was in use as an overflow to Chiswick Works. *John Gillham*

Above:
The preserved Chiswick Power Station, which once generated power for electric trams, forms an impressive backdrop to a more mundane Fleetline working as a training bus from Stamford Brook, as the garage is now known. *John Gillham*

In 1978 work started on an improvement scheme (to cost £1 million) which would allow the Riverside (R) allocation and staff to move here temporarily while a new garage was built at Hammersmith. After that was finished it was planned to move the Turnham Green allocation here and close that garage. However, by the time the Chiswick premises reopened in 1980 as Stamford Brook, the Riverside/Hammersmith plan had been dropped. A new office block had been built, and property adjoining the entrance had been demolished to allow it to be widened; all told the cost was said to be £2 million. There was an official opening in April, but the garage did not come into use until May, when 45 buses (RMs, Ms and LSs) and 210 staff, all from Turnham Green, started work; the 'new' garage also inherited the 'V' code, despite its rather different location.

The airport connection was revived in November 1980, when, the day after British Airways ceased operating its former BOAC service between Victoria and Heathrow, Stamford Brook began running Ms with extra luggage space and fewer seats on new routes A1 and A2 from Heathrow to Central London. A few years later a newer batch of Ms was fitted with Voith four-speed gearboxes and coach seats for the routes, which involved motorway running.

In 1994 some 91 vehicles were scheduled from the garage, including 26 Ms on the A1 and A2. The rest of the fleet comprised three MRLs, 18 Ms, 19 Ls (Leyland-bodied Leyland Olympians) and 25 DTs (Dennis Darts with the original Dartline-style bodies). Soon afterwards, however, the buses for the A1 and A2 were moved, being based at the West Ramp at Heathrow, though servicing was still done at Stamford Brook. In November 1996 the garage closed and became a store for unlicensed vehicles, but it

reopened in October 1999 when a number of routes were reallocated. By mid-2001 it had a scheduled requirement for 37 buses — almost all Dennis Darts, including one in Marks & Spencer colours for a shuttle service between the M&S store in Kew and Richmond town centre.

TOLWORTH (TR)
by Tolworth railway station

When Kingston garage finally closed — for demolition — in 2000, buses moved to a temporary base, pending the opening of a new 90-bus depot at Tolworth, originally expected in July 2000. A recruitment centre for the garage was opened in Tolworth Broadway in March 2001, but the revised depot opening date of June 2001 was also not achieved; it opened in November 2001.

WOOD LANE (B)
Wood Lane, on London Underground's
White City complex

London United opened a depot on part of this site in July 1992, initially for buses on route 9A; later, route 72 was also transferred there. It was an outstation for Shepherd's Bush, with buses visiting the latter for refuelling and washing. The garage code B was chosen because it was the original code for Shepherd's Bush before the old alphabetical code system was revised, though it had been in use until recently for Battersea.

Wood Lane operated some 33 DR-class Dennis Darts. The base closed at the end of March 1995, the buses and their workings transferring to Shepherd's Bush.

METROLINE

Metroline was the subject of an employee/management buy-out in October 1994. It later took over London Northern from MTL, while more recently the Metroline group was acquired by DelGro of Singapore.

CRICKLEWOOD (W)
Edgware Road, Cricklewood

Dollis Hill (Cricklewood) must have been quite a place to be in the earliest days of the motor bus. It was then rather remote from London, but in 1905 the London Power Omnibus Company began one of the first regular motor-bus services in the capital. It also built a bus garage which it claimed to be Europe's largest. The garage was probably never very full, and voluntary liquidation followed in 1907.

The LGOC had built stables in the same vicinity in 1898, and one shed was converted to a motor-bus garage in 1905; it was known originally as Dollis Hill

and only later as Cricklewood garage. It was the first motorised depot used by the LGOC.

Early motor-bus operations were unprofitable and chaotic, with different makes being tried, with varying degrees of success. By mid-1907, affairs at Cricklewood were so chaotic that Col Frank Searle was transferred from his post as Superintendent at Mortlake garage to the chief depot, Cricklewood. Here, he later said, he found a state of affairs far more amazing than those at Mortlake. 'At Cricklewood we were blessed with 28 types of vehicle, and about 300 horses, together with their horse buses under the same roof. You can imagine the good fellowship with which the horse and the motor sections pulled together — the proverbial cat and dog life must have been heaven by comparison.' For horse-bus drivers, grooms, farriers and all the other horse-bus staff would have felt their jobs threatened by the new motor bus.

Searle had barely settled in when the manager of the LGOC's motor department left and Searle became Chief Engineer, at a salary of £450 a year. The job

Below:
The rear of the offices and canteen are on the right of this 1976 picture of Cricklewood, while the front running shed is on the left. *John Gillham*

included taking charge of the whole motor-bus fleet of 145 vehicles, but he also had to continue as manager responsible for Cricklewood.

Buses which have worked from the garage included the blue-liveried Daimlers of the Tramways (MET) Omnibus Company from January 1913 and an experimental town-gas-powered bus of 1918 intended as a prototype for a small fleet at a time of petrol shortages. The first batch of open-stair LTs was allocated here for route 121 from January 1930, but later that year STs replaced them. The garage eventually became the base for all the LS class buses for route 16A (Cricklewood–Victoria), the last of which ran in the early months of 1937. Just before the outbreak of World War 2 the garage was operating STL-, T- and Q-type buses.

During 1921, just before Chiswick opened, Cricklewood had been one of the four LGOC garages to undertake chassis and mechanical parts overhauls. In 1940/1 it undertook body overhauls.

From 1949 to 1954 the garage operated the largest allocation of SRTs — on route 16, which had a scheduled requirement for 68. All told, it operated some 90 out of the total fleet of 160, though of course not all at the same time. At times it had RTs, then RTLs, then RTs again, and then over about 10 years almost all the rear-engined single-deck types, plus DMSs and, later,

Ms, as well as RMLs. Its association with Ms began early, as from October 1978 it received the five pre-production buses. A more illustrious prototype had been RM1, which first saw public service from the garage on route 2 in 1956.

The garage appeared to face an uncertain future at the start of the 1990s, but subsequently saw its workload increase considerably. After Metroline Holdings bought Brents Coaches in 1995, Metroline Travel's own coaches were moved from Cricklewood to Brents' base at Watford. Today route 16 needs just 16 buses — all low-floor Alexander-bodied Dennis Tridents. The garage has a total scheduled requirement for some 90 buses, but route 16 is no longer the busiest route; that distinction goes to the 189, with 18 DLDs — 10.1m Dennis Dart SLFs with Plaxton Pointer 2 dual-door bodywork.

EDGWARE (EW)
Station Road, Edgware

As if to emphasise how difficult it is to judge how an area will grow, the current Edgware garage is really the third to be built. The first was opened by the LGOC in 1925 adjoining the recently-extended Edgware Underground station. There was room for 24 buses, though there was

Below:
Spare land by Edgware garage was used in the 1950s for storing buses ready for the tram-replacement schemes and later for storing surplus buses. Here an STL and some prewar STDs await their fate. *Author*

Above:
A mix of tired-looking AEC Swifts and some smart new Bristol LHs are present in this 1977 view of the second garage built at Edgware. *Capital Transport*

Below:
The second garage is still in use in this picture, with a fleet of Metrobuses and LHs, while garage number three rises in the background. *Bill Godwin*

space for expansion. In January 1939 a new building was completed alongside the original, with space for open parking, and the earlier garage then became the bus station. The parking space was used for storing many of the new buses for tram-replacement schemes and also for storing redundant buses prior to sale a little later.

Some internal reconstruction work was carried out in the early 1960s, but a new and larger garage was planned in the 1970s. Work began in 1982 on a derelict site that once contained the British Rail station and sidings adjacent to the Underground station. To minimise noise levels in a mainly residential area the new garage is sunk 10ft into the ground. It opened in October 1984, having cost £4.5 million, and had space for 100 buses.

In 1992, with Cricklewood set to become a fully functional garage again (rather than just a running shed, with few facilities), Metroline announced the closure of Edgware, with a new midibus base to be set up in the car park and front yard outside the garage. This took place in March 1993, and bus washing, fuelling and other facilities were provided in the yard.

In 1999 Sovereign had won tenders for route 114 (again), all its Harrow operations and also for the 183, a route previously operated by Metroline. From May that year, Sovereign took a 10-year lease on half of the garage and spent £250,000 on providing a 24-hour maintenance facility and refurbishing the garage and office accommodation; at the same time it closed its former BTS base at Borehamwood.

More surprising, perhaps, is that Metroline moved back into the other half of the garage in September 2000, making it one of the very few London garages to be shared by two operators.

Over the years, Edgware has seen a fair variety of vehicles. In August 1938 it was running STs and STLs, plus LT single-deckers. The year 1949 saw the first postwar buses, with RTWs and TDs; the TDs were long-lived, being finally replaced on the 240A — the last London route worked by the type — in October 1962. RTLs joined RTWs in 1950, but both were subsequently ousted by RTs, which remained until 1973 when DMSs took over. RFs had replaced the TDs and remained until 1977 when replaced by BLs. SMSs ran in some numbers from 1970 to 1981 but were replaced by double-deckers. Postwar allocations had generally been fairly static in terms of total fleet, for example 62 scheduled buses in 1952 and 55 in 1987.

In mid-2001 Sovereign had the slightly larger allocation, with a scheduled requirement for 63 vehicles. Eighteen RMLs were required for route 13 (though these were starting to be replaced by refurbished RMs), 21 Leyland/Volvo Olympians for routes 114 and 292, another five, older Olympians or Titans for school and other workings and 19 low-floor Dennis Dart SLFs with Plaxton Pointer 2 bodies for routes H12 and 183.

Metroline was operating 27 Ms on two double-deck routes, plus 23 low-floor Dennis Dart SLFs with Plaxton Pointer 2 bodies (EDRs) and eight similar Darts but with two-door bodies, on seven routes altogether.

HARLESDEN (HR/RI*)
Atlas Road, Harlesden

The Atlas Road site was inherited from Atlas Bus in 1994 and has had a chequered career but became increasingly important. Metroline had bought Watford-based Brents Travel Group in 1995, but after more than two years moved the fleet here. Subsequently a number of buses were also stored on the site, including the withdrawn but youthful LN-class Dennis Lances, which proved difficult to sell.

Closure of the North Acton base on 26 September 2000 saw buses start their day from there and finish at Harlesden, which became a main operating centre again, the LN class by this time having been sold.

HARROW WEALD (HD)
High Road, Chapel Hill, Harrow Weald

The LGOC had a small garage at South Harrow, adjoining the Underground station. It opened in 1925 with room for six buses but soon became too small. Its replacement was a new, larger building in High Road, Harrow Weald. This opened in April 1930 but had to be extended just two years later by building forwards over the forecourt. All told the garage cost £21,000.

Harrow Weald soon became the garage to which the LGOC allocated experimental vehicles. The company bought three Daimler CH6s with Daimler sleeve-valve petrol engines (with a prodigious oil consumption) in order to test in service the chassis's use of fluid flywheel and preselector gearbox. The buses arrived in 1931 and were withdrawn four years later, but the combination of fluid flywheel and preselector 'box was to become standard for the London fleet for many years. The garage also housed the LGOC's first diesel-engined buses — three STs — though they soon reverted to petrol engines. Two double-deck, side-engined Q-type buses (surely a design ahead of its time) were also based there.

By the outbreak of World War 2 the garage had a mixed fleet of ST and STL double-deckers and C and Q single-deckers. Heavy wartime traffic on route 230 prompted the allocation from October 1942 of some lowbridge STLs — standard chassis which were re-bodied with Chiswick-built low-height bodies finished to a wartime specification to replace the Q single-deckers, as did a couple of elderly low-height STs later converted to diesel. They lasted until 1952, when low-height RLHs — AEC Regents with Weymann provincial-style bodies — replaced them. In the early postwar years RTWs and SRTs spent brief periods here, before being ousted by RTs. TDs arrived in 1949 and lasted for five years, after which no single-deckers were operated until 1966 when a couple of RFs arrived for new route 136. MBs came in 1970 and SMSs the following year, at which time most routes became one-person-operated. Both the MBs and some MBSs which had followed left in 1976, with SMSs lingering in

Above:
A conventional single-decker and a low-floor double-decker stand ready for their next journeys from Harrow Weald while driving staff likewise sit ready on a bench outside. *Author*

declining numbers until 1979, when LSs took over all single-deck duties. The RMs which replaced RTs in 1978 were replaced by Ms in 1983, and these Metrobuses were later used to convert a number of routes back to double-deck operation.

In May 1952 the peak vehicle requirement was for 87 buses, but this had fallen to 60 by early 1987. However, the open parking space at the rear had been enlarged in 1970.

November 1987 saw the establishment of Harrow Buses, an autonomous unit set up within London Buses which, having won tenders for a local network, began operating from the garage. Its fleet comprised a mixture of new and elderly buses, the new including new leased MCW Metrobuses plus 26 ex-West Midlands Travel Ailsas. Smaller vehicles included 30 MCW Metroriders, which were actually kept at an outstation at East Lane, North Wembley. However, the low-cost unit was not a success, and most of the work was lost on re-tender.

Despite the demise of Harrow Buses, the garage itself managed to survive and by May 1994 was running some 40 Metrobuses plus about a dozen Dennis Darts. In mid-2001 the fleet based there was rather more

modern, and met a scheduled requirement for 36 low-floor double-deckers (all Dennis Tridents with Alexander bodies) and five Dennis Dart SLFs with Plaxton Pointer 2 bodies. Finally, for route 186 were 12 LLW-class Dennis Lance SLFs with Wright Pathfinder bodies; new in 1994 these were some of the last buses ordered by LT before privatisation and also represented its first pioneering steps in introducing low-floor buses. The garage also undertakes engineering work on buses based at North Wembley and Edgware, which are outstations for engineering purposes.

NORTH WEMBLEY (NW)
GEC Estate, East Lane, Wembley

This site came into use before the buy-out of the company in 1994 and was then a midibus base. As with most midibuses, the vehicles allocated have tended to increase in length as new tenders have been awarded, and those forming the 2001 allocation are probably better described as single-deckers. Maintenance on vehicles based here is carried out at Harrow Weald garage.

Above:
Two Metrobuses occupy the doorway at Willesden garage in 1991. A War Memorial to staff can be seen on the right.
Kevin Lane

WILLESDEN (AC)
High Road and Pound Lane, Willesden

The original Willesden garage was opened in 1912, later becoming one of the four garages used for overhaul of chassis and mechanical parts before Chiswick Works opened in 1921. Later, during World War 2, it undertook body overhauls. Just before the outbreak of that war its allocation consisted of STs and STLs.

Postwar double-deckers were RTs, which began to arrive in 1948, and RTWs, which followed in 1951. The RTs were displaced by RTLs in 1955 but then ousted the RTLs in 1968, Willesden being the last garage to operate the Leylands. From January 1958 the garage had operated the third prototype Routemaster — RML3, as it was then numbered — on route 8. It went on to run the first production RMs allocated for passenger service, with two on route 8 from June 1959; they moved on for trolleybus replacement in November that year. RMs reappeared at the garage in 1965 to replace the RTWs, RMLs following the next year. However, RTs lasted until 1976 and RMs until 1986. SMSs had arrived in 1970 for route 226, being replaced by DMSs in 1978. Metrobuses came in 1980, displacing the DMSs, and by 1986 some 40 were allocated.

Improvements to the garage were authorised in 1974 at an estimated cost of £804,000; work started early in 1975 and enlarged its capacity from 90 to 120 buses. There had been talk of also building 40 'units of housing' for staff, but nothing seems to have come of this proposal. It had been said that, when the work was completed, Stonebridge garage would close, but this did not happen either: Stonebridge work and crews ultimately moved to the new Westbourne Park garage.

One of the routes lost in tendering had been the 52, but in November 1994 Metroline became the first ex-London Buses company to expand when it bought Atlas Bus & Coach from the Pullmans Group. Some 26 Ts and 80 staff for the 52 and N52 continued under the Atlas name until September 1996, but the route was moved back to Willesden from the former Atlas depot at Harlesden in November 1995.

Back in 1994 the garage had been operating 43 RMLs, 23 Ms and 11 LNs (Dennis Lances with Northern Counties Paladin bodies), plus 16 Dennis Darts. Seven years later there were still 43 scheduled RMLs (for routes 6 and 98), but the 52 had gained 24 VPLs (10.6m low-floor Volvo B7TLs with Plaxton President bodies). Low-floor single-deckers were 25 DLDs (10.1m Dennis Dart/Plaxton Pointer 2s). The schedules also required 14 AVs (Volvo Olympians with Alexander bodies), making a total of 106 buses.

Above:
The trams had gone and some buses had arrived (for storage) when this picture of what was officially Highgate depot was taken in 1952, but trolleybuses still had another eight years to go — some are just visible on the far left. Note the tram track in the floor. *John Gillham*

Below:
The traverser survived after the trolleybuses went, though it can no longer traverse, as the area on either side has been concreted in this 1961 view of Holloway. *John Gillham*

METROLINE LONDON NORTHERN

London Northern was bought by MTL Trust Holdings in October 1994. It became known as MTL London, and was acquired by Metroline Holdings in 1998.

HOLLOWAY (HT)
(Highgate from 1950 to 1971)
Pemberton Gardens, Holloway

A double change of identity has occurred here. This garage was originally Holloway tram depot, but was renamed Highgate in 1950 to avoid confusion with Holloway bus garage (code J). Following closure of the latter in 1971, this former tram — later trolleybus — depot resumed its former name of Holloway.

It was opened by the LCC in November 1907 and had space for 336 trams to make it the undertaking's largest depot. It had a total of 52 tracks, laid on either side of the traverser which ran the full width of the car shed. Conversion from tram operation proved to be a protracted affair, as the first trolleybuses started running from the depot in March 1938 but the last trams continued until April 1952, surviving tram routes being the 33 and 35, both running through the Kingsway Subway.

Even the trolleybus-to-bus changeover was made in more than one stage, with the first route converted in July 1960 and the last in April 1961. The conversion was unique in London in that for a time a Sundays-only working by the depot on the 609, otherwise worked entirely by Finchley depot, continued after RMs had arrived. These carried the route number 609 and ran alongside the Finchley trolleybus allocation on the service.

February 1961 saw the biggest part of the changeover when 117 RMs were allocated, and when it was finally completed there was an allocation of 156 RMs. A number of RTLs were allocated from 1963 to 1965 and then replaced by RTs. The evaluation exercise to compare rear-engined buses with Routemasters saw XAs (Leyland Atlanteans) allocated to route 271 from January 1966, displacing RMs. Later, eight of the XAs were exchanged with all eight XFs (Fleetlines) in the Country Area, and from April 1966 these green buses were also compared. Then, in the July, Holloway received RMLs for the 271, passing on its XAs and returning the XFs to the Country Area.

The garage was enlarged and had extra maintenance facilities added to allow it to take the vehicles and operations from nearby Holloway (code J) garage when that closed in September 1971. It then had a peak of some 210 buses. The figure again drifted downwards subsequently, but in July 1993, when Chalk Farm closed and five more routes and their vehicles were added to its allocation, Holloway once again became the largest garage in London.

Not all the garage's operations were with large buses. In 1975 it received the first BS (Bristol LHS/ECW) buses in the fleet to replace Ford Transits on the C11; in 1981 the allocation altered to the larger BL after some changes in the roads covered to allow for the longer buses.

The garage kept up its large allocation and in May 1994 was running 164 scheduled vehicles, of which 79 were Ms and the remainder a mix of Dennis Darts and smaller vehicles. The mid-2001 total amounted to some 200 scheduled buses of 10 different types. The largest class was the TP (low-floor Dennis Trident/Plaxton President), numbering 36, while there were also 27 of the rival low-floor offering of VPLs (Volvo B7TLs with Plaxton President bodies). Less exciting double-deckers were a combined total of 26 Ms and Vs (Metrobuses and Volvo Olympians) and 24 RMLs. Single-deckers totalled 40 step-entrance Dennis Darts with various makes of bodywork, 25 DLDs (Dart SLFs with Plaxton Pointer 2 bodies) and finally seven MRLs (Optare MetroRiders).

NORTH ACTON (NA)
Victoria Road, North Acton

When, in 1995, MTL took over R&I Tours (trading as R&I Buses and R&I Coaches), along with a fleet of over 60 vehicles, it also acquired the R&I premises in North Acton, plus a nearby maintenance base in Western Road, Park Royal.

Both sites continued in use after Metroline acquired London Northern from MTL, but the lease on the North Acton premises expired in 2000; buses then moved to the former Atlas Bus depot in Harlesden.

North Acton's allocations were totally single-deck, but were nevertheless of considerable variety, including as they did MAN 11.220s with either Optare Vecta or Marshall bodywork.

POTTERS BAR (PB)
High Street, Potters Bar

This garage was built by the LGOC for the associated company Overground and opened in May 1930. It cost £48,348 and was set back from the High Street in Potters Bar, a town that was then in Middlesex but in the 1960s 'moved' to Hertfordshire. At a fairly early stage it was realised that it was too far north of the red bus network and there were thoughts of closure. Back in the 1930s the garage was described as being three

miles beyond Hadley Highstone, then the terminal of Overground's main route, and calculations were made as to how many crews could be saved by a move. More recently, in the early deregulated era of the 1980s, there was again threat of closure, but, perhaps helped by a revised pay agreement, the garage has survived; in June 1986 it won a Hertfordshire CC contract from London Country for the 84 (St Albans–New Barnet) and also a joint Herts/LRT contract for the 263 (Potters Bar/ Arkley–Archway).

At the outbreak of war the whole allocation was of STs. After the war spare space was used to store buses awaiting conversion back to peacetime duties, while later it stored STLs being held ready for extra Festival of Britain services, once Poplar trolleybus depot was full. Later still, part of the garage was leased to Arlington, the coach dealership.

During the war the garage was allocated a number of open-stair LTs — an unkind choice for its rather long routes. It gained some new STDs late in 1946, but for some reason did not take kindly to them; they soon moved to Loughton, and Potters Bar had to wait (or perhaps chose to wait) until 1947 for new RTs. Ultimately it became an all-RT garage, with a maximum requirement for 68 in 1952. By 1966 the total output had fallen to 48 — a mix of RTs and RMs. In 1973 the one and only FRM was allocated for one-bus route 284, lasting until 1976. Later, a pair of Ford minibuses began operating new local service PB1 (a revamped 284) from 1977, and were replaced by two not very successful A-class Dodges in 1983. These lasted until June 1986, when the route was lost under a Herts CC tendering scheme. Less unusual

buses, meanwhile, for more mainstream work, had been RFs (briefly), then MBs followed by SMSs. Crew-operated DMSs and later one-person DMSs arrived from late 1973, initially to replace RMs, but the latter made a brief comeback nine years later.

The late 1980s saw an amazing (for LT) mix of buses. These included secondhand Metrobuses from Greater Manchester, Yorkshire Rider and Busways — all single-door versions, two of the Yorkshire buses having Alexander bodywork. Then there were Ailsas — 12 ex-South Yorkshire, with unusual Van Hool-McArdle bodies, plus 24 of a big batch of Alexander-bodied buses bought from West Midlands. Transfers within the fleet also brought the three Alisas bought new as part of LT's Alternative Vehicle Evaluation trials. Rather more popular, no doubt, were the nine new Alexander-bodied Scania double-deckers (S class) bought new by LT in 1989. In December 1993, after Finchley garage closed, the X43 (the pioneer limited-stop service along London's first Red Route) also moved to Potters Bar, along with its specially liveried Scania double-deckers. These also appeared on Saturdays on the 84.

In early 2001 the fleet still included more than 20 Ms (a type which first arrived in 1981), two different lengths of Dennis Dart with Plaxton Pointer bodywork, and two different lengths of Dennis Dart SLF with Marshall bodywork. All told, these Darts meet a scheduled requirement for 20 step-entrance versions (types DRL and EDR) and 43 low-floor versions (types DML and DMS). With a total requirement for 84 buses, this is more than double the number of buses working from the garage 14 years ago.

Above:
Van Hool-McArdle-bodied Ailsas — unusual in London — predominate in this view at the garage in 1988. *Author*

Below:
One of the many secondhand buses added to the fleet at Potters Bar, an Ailsa stands by the fuelling island
in the entrance to the garage in 1990. *Author*

STAGECOACH EAST LONDON

East London was sold to Stagecoach in September 1994, being known thereafter as Stagecoach East London.

BARKING (BK)
Longbridge Road

Barking will be long remembered by most enthusiasts as the last garage to operate RTs, until 7 April 1979. More recently, the new TAs (low-floor Dennis Tridents with Alexander ALX400 bodies) delivered in 1999 were the first new double-deckers to be allocated since 1980.

It was the LCC's new housing estates in the Becontree area of Essex that increased demand for bus services after World War 1. The existing LGOC garages at Poplar (Athol Street), Forest Gate, Upton Park and Seven Kings did not have surplus capacity, so the LGOC built a new garage at Barking, which opened in January 1924. Only seven years later it was extended and modernised. For a time in the 1930s it was known as Fair Cross garage.

In the run-up to World War 2 Barking's sole allocation had been LTs, but it subsequently gained a large allocation of utility Gs. Among routes they worked was the 23, then running well into Central London from Becontree Heath. Even in the difficult times just after the war, the route had an allocation of 46 Gs, and the continued rostering of these into the 1950s was to become a sore point with staff. However, the garage received some postwar buses quite early, with an allocation of RTLs arriving in 1949: as a class they

lasted until 1958 when RTs took over. There were also small numbers of RTWs and SRTs. The allocation of RMs from 1964 to 1970 was quite small, but this class then replaced the last RTs.

Most routes gained DMSs from mid-1972 onwards, but Ts replaced them from 1980, when the RMs also went. Single-deckers at the garage were limited to RFs from 1965 to 1974 and SMSs from 1971 to 1974, in each case on just one route.

The total scheduled requirement had fallen steadily from 140 buses in 1952 to 83 in 1987, and a closure announcement was made in 1992 because of loss of routes under tendering; happily, it was not implemented. By May 1994 the scheduled allocation was up to 109 buses, including 41 Ts and 24 of the striking Optare-bodied DAF SB220s better known as Optare Deltas (DA class). Smaller buses included classes of Dennis Dart totalling 44 buses. The mid-2001 allocation totalled 118, comprising 28 Ts and 14 DAs, plus 16 TAs (Dennis Trident/Alexanders), 32 PDs (step-entrance Dart/Plaxtons) and 28 SLDs (low-floor Dart SLFs with Plaxton Pointer 2 bodies).

BOW (BW)
Fairfield Road, Bow

Bow is one of several London bus garages that originated as a tram depot and later saw trolleybus operations before being converted for a third form of

Above:
The 1920s style of Barking garage is clearly evident in this mid-1960s view. The single-storey building between the two doorways has since been removed. *Gerald Mead*

Above:
The driver of a low-height Volvo Olympian chats to a colleague as his bus stands in the main doorway of the former municipal tram depot at Bow. *Author*

Below:
The spacious interior of Bow garage harbours a variety of types. The stanchions supporting the roof can be clearly seen — and are clearly marked. *Author*

traction. It was built by the LCC on the site of Grove Hall Asylum, which had been bought for £6,000. The first section came into use in 1908 with (as planned) a second section added two years later; that part was used for bodywork maintenance on the LCC's growing fleet.

The depot was duly reconstructed for trolleybuses, which arrived in November 1939. It had an official capacity of 102 vehicles and a maximum scheduled requirement of 98.

Conversion to take buses included installation of four 5,000gal above-ground fuel tanks, removal of the traverser and filling of its pit, and adapting the pits at the eastern end of the garage. Some 61 RTLs were allocated to Bow, while most of its trolleybuses were comparatively modern and were reallocated to four other depots.

When Clay Hall garage (just a couple of streets away but the wrong side of a low bridge) closed in November

1959 — just three months after Bow became a bus garage — most of its routes moved here, with their crews and buses, making it the only former trolleybus depot to run RTWs: it received 37 of them plus five RTLs. Among the work transferred was one bus (an RTL) on the Port of London Authority's Custom House–Manor Way service.

By 1966 the fleet consisted of RTLs and RMs, while 10 years later it was a mix of RMs, RMLs and DMSs. By early 1987 it comprised both types of Routemaster and LSs; the RMLs are still there today, for route 8, with a scheduled requirement of 25. Two lengths of Dennis Trident/Alexander feature: there are eight 10m TASs for route 241, while route 26 sees 10.5m TA versions intermixed with VA-class Alexander-bodied Volvo Olympians; the latter also work two other routes in their entirety. The garage's total peak output requires 77 buses.

Above:
Buses ran around for years carrying the code for the Chadwell Heath depot, which would have looked like this but was never built. *Author's collection*

CHADWELL HEATH (CH)
Freshwater Road, Chadwell Heath

This is a garage that never was, despite the fact that buses ran around for some four years displaying its garage code. London Buses bought the land for its East London subsidiary in 1992, the intention being to build a garage or depot with open parking for 250 buses, full maintenance facilities and a canteen for 600 people (though not all at once!). There was also to be a new head office. Tenders for three routes were won based on operations from the new depot from March 1993, and buses based at Barking and North Street, Romford, which were to close, began to gain CH codes. Seven Kings was also to close, but in the end was the only garage that actually did.

First there were delays in gaining planning permission, and then the site was found to be heavily contaminated from when it was a paint warehouse. Ultimately the plan was abandoned altogether.

LEYTON (T)
Leyton Green Road and High Road, Leyton

Leyton Garage was built by the LGOC in 1912 to replace another in the area acquired from the Great Eastern London Motor Omnibus Company. It was in a good situation for services to Epping Forest as well as those along the roads also served by the municipal tramways in the area. At the outbreak of World War 2 it had an allocation of LTs and STs, but by the end of 1940 it was working a large number of open-stair LTs on four routes.

London's first serious wartime loss of buses was of 10 Tilling STs (also open-stair) during the early part of the Blitz; ironically they had been parked at a dispersal site as part of a scheme to avoid the risk of having too many buses parked together. The bodies were scrapped but some of the chassis were sold to the Home Guard. Later the garage itself was damaged by bombing, reconstruction not being completed until the late 1950s, major renovation having started in 1955.

Above and below:
Leyton garage seen on two different dates in 1975. Routemasters and a Fleetline occupy one picture while more Routemasters and a Merlin dominate the other. *Gerald Mead; John Gillham*

The garage gained the first postwar RTs, the very first, Weymann-bodied RT402, going into service on route 10 on 10 May 1947, to be followed by the first Park Royal-bodied example, RT152, on 23 May. By October the garage had 78 RTs and all the open-stair LTs had moved away. RTs did not finally depart until 1972. The second stage of the trolleybus conversion scheme in April 1959 added 30 more RTs to Leyton's fleet, making it London's second-largest garage.

From 1949 the single-deck allocation was TDs, replaced by RFs in 1958. Conversion of route 236 (jointly operated with Dalston garage) to one-person-operated SMSs in April 1971 brought to an end crew operation of RFs in the Central Area. The growing single-deck fleet at the garage included MBs, then SMs and SMDs, these giving way to LSs in 1978/9. Titans

arrived in mid-1987, but at that time there was still a large crew-operated fleet, with 35 RMLs required for the 38 and another 17 for the 55.

By 1994 the garage was operating only the 38 on Sundays using 15 Titans, while a different London Buses company, Leaside, was running the route on weekdays. Leyton was working seven routes all told, with a fleet of more than 80 Ts. Five years later, in January 1999, Stagecoach East London put its first low-floor double-decker, a Dennis Trident with Alexander ALX400 body, into service from the garage. Some two years on, the garage's TA fleet totals well over 70 for five different routes. With 12 SLDs (Dennis Dart SLFs with Alexander ALX200 bodies) for route 230, the entire fleet at Leyton is made up of low-floor buses.

Above:
One of the short-lived SRT class leaves the newly-opened but not quite finished North Street, Romford, garage. *Author*

NORTH STREET, ROMFORD (NS)
North Street, Seymer Road and Park Drive, Romford

Opened in August 1953, the new garage in North Street was designed to take pressure off the overcrowded Hornchurch (RD) garage that had had to cope with a general expansion of services and also the building of the huge postwar Harold Hill estate. The new garage was designed to LT's postwar pattern, with a one-way flow through the garage starting at the refuelling and cleaning islands in the usual style. Both entrance and exit were via side roads and not on or off the busy North Street itself.

The imposing exterior was in tube-station style, with a small tower over the staircase complete with traditional 'bullseye' above tall vertical windows. The offices and facilities fronted the main road, with the two-storey office block to the left of the tower. The 285ft by 120ft parking area could take 115 buses.

The garage began with nine routes needing a scheduled 67 buses, for which 47 were transferred from

Hornchurch and others from Barking, Forest Gate and Seven Kings. The main type was STL (36 buses), followed by the RTL (20), the unpopular SRT (10) and finally the TD (5). More work was passed to the garage in February 1954, from Upton Park. The same year, RTs replaced the RTLs and then the STLs and SRTs.

Work at the garage continued to grow, with an allocation of over 90 in early 1958, but then began to decline. RFs replaced the TDs in 1959, RMs arrived in 1966 and SMSs in 1971. DMSs gradually replaced the SMSs, the last of which went in 1976 when the first BLs to enter service with LT arrived in April. Ts started replacing DMSs from November 1979, while LSs replaced the BLs in January 1980.

A more eye-catching conversion was on the 175s at the height of LT's bus shortages, when former British Airways forward-entrance Routemasters (RMAs) took over from RTs. The RMAs had minimal destination and route-number displays and many were still in BA colours; they ran from October 1975 to September

1976. Another strange situation occurred on Sundays in 1988, when route 66 was operated by a mixture of double-deckers (Ts) and midibuses (MR-class Metroriders).

Closure was announced by East London in 1992 because of loss of routes in tendering, but the garage remained open. By May 1994 it required 84 buses for scheduled operations: a mix of 72 Ts and 10 DRLs (Plaxton Pointer-bodied Dennis Darts) plus two LSs for Mobility Bus routes.

In mid-2001 the scheduled vehicle requirement was for 89 buses, route allocations being somewhat mixed. Five routes were worked by a combination of Titans and Northern Counties-bodied Volvo Olympians (VNs), accounting for 46 buses altogether. What might be called 'pure' Titan operation involved a surprising nine Ts for three schooldays-only routes numbered in the 600s, plus four for a Ford contract. Trunk route 86 was operated with 18 TAs (low-floor Dennis Trident/Alexander ALX400) plus a further two Ts on school-days, and one route (247) needed seven SLDs (low-floor Dennis Darts) and three more Ts.

STRATFORD (SD)
Waterden Road, Stratford

This depot opened in September 1992 and consists of a large yard and part of an existing industrial building. It seems to have had difficulty in coming to terms with its location, since it was originally called the Bow midibus base, and took over all the midibuses previously operated by Bow and West Ham garages. More recently, Dennis Darts have been based here in quantity, including some in blue or green livery for services from London City Airport to Liverpool Street or Canning Town respectively. The depot is now known as Stratford and is situated in a mixed industrial area not far from

the M11 motorway and Stratford's rail-dominated hinterland. In the same road, and just metres away on the opposite side, is First Capital's Hackney depot, while destination blinds of the one bus route to the location describe it as Hackney Wick.

UPTON PARK (U)
Redclyffe Road, Upton Park

This was for many years the largest garage in the fleet, with an allocation of more than 200 buses. In terms of vehicles operated it has also been one of the most interesting. For many years it was well-known to enthusiasts for its habit of also having fleet numbers on the rear dome of the buses because the running shift offices were at a high level above the garage entrance.

The garage was originally opened by the London Road Car Company in 1907. It was requisitioned in November 1915 and did not reopen until May 1919. Later it was completely renewed and enlarged at a total cost of £120,000, coming back into use in October 1931. It now had a capacity of 200-plus buses, with an overhead refuelling system and a parking area entirely free of stanchions. Its scheduled requirement was for 155 buses, and by early 1932 it had received 157 LT-type double-deckers and seven LT single-deckers.

Upton Park's nicely standardised fleet of virtually new buses was to be spoiled from January 1934 when all the acquired double-deck Leyland Titans in the Central bus fleet (except for a few diesel-engined examples) were moved there. They came from a variety of operators, had bodies by several builders and were less than ideal for conductors, since interior layouts varied and there were big variations in the height of the step from the platform into the lower deck. First withdrawals of the Titans came in late 1937, though many were later

Above:
Routemasters dominate this 2001 view of the large Upton Park garage. The docking area is on the right. *Author*

returned to service for a while; however, the remaining 30 were withdrawn at the end of September 1939, the final home for these buses having been the incredibly frequent route 101. In June 1939, meanwhile, all the garage's diesel-engined STLs had been exchanged for petrol-engined versions from Clay Hall.

Between October 1940 and March 1941, after LT had appealed to provincial operators for help, Upton Park received two former London Titans on loan from Young's Motor Services of Paisley: one was a former Country Area bus while the other had previously been allocated to Upton Park! In March 1945 a V2 rocket which fell on nearby buildings did serious damage to 15 delicensed Tilling STs stored outside, and 14 of them had to be scrapped.

The garage was the last in the fleet to be allocated utility Guy Arabs, not receiving its first until November 1945, but had 80 by April 1946 and 107 by the end of 1950. Another example of how quickly a large organisation can expedite matters is demonstrated by the demise of the garage's LT-type double-deckers: on 1 January 1950 it still had 41, of which nine were still running on the 11th, but all had gone by 12 January, being replaced by surplus STLs transferred in.

One particularly interesting operation with LTs had been introduced in November 1947, when 19 open-stair examples were put on to an LNER (later BR Eastern Region) service to replace trains on the Woodford loop via Ilford and Roding Valley while the line was rebuilt for the forthcoming Central Line Underground extension. The service called at seven intermediate stations but was cut back as the extension gradually opened, finally ending in November 1948, when the last six open-stair LTs were transferred elsewhere.

RTs had arrived in 1948 and RTWs in 1950, these types ultimately forming the bulk of the allocation. But the Gs were not finally replaced until December 1952, when the last was withdrawn from route 101; back in 1947 this had a Saturday requirement for 71 Gs and five years later was still a highly intensive service.

It was STLs that aided the replacement of the Gs, with a batch being moved in, for example, after the Festival of Britain services finished. The last STLs in Central Area service finished on 29 June 1954, and again these were Upton Park buses on the 101. RTs on the same route were replaced by RMs in late 1972.

The last vehicles to be ordered by London Buses were 30 low-floor Scania single-deckers with Wright bodies, and 16 of these SLWs were delivered to Upton Park in November 1994 — many for route 101 where they replaced Titans (of the modern variety!). By this time, however, the East London company was owned by Stagecoach.

One unusual operation worthy of note was the introduction of the X15 Beckton Express in March 1988, operated by six smartly refurbished former Green Line RMC Routemasters in a special red and gold livery. Newspapers were sold on board this commuter service, which ran into Central London in the mornings and back (from Trafalgar Square) in the afternoons.

Some three RMCs were still at work from the garage in mid-2001, plus five RMs and numerous RMLs to provide the 24 buses required for route 15, and there is still a need for 16 SLWs on the 101. Only the Routemasters are not low-floor, the remaining requirements being fulfilled by Alexander-bodied Dennis buses; the double-deckers comprise 24 10.5m TA and 13 10m TAS Tridents, and single-deckers 28 SLD low-floor Darts. The total requirement is identical to that in May 1994, though one-person-operated double-deckers then consisted of 24 Ts and 36 Ss (Scanias) while single-deckers were a mix of Dennis Darts, Optare MetroRiders and Optare StarRider-bodied Mercedes-Benz 811Ds.

STAGECOACH SELKENT

Selkent was bought by Stagecoach in September 1994.

BROMLEY (TB)
Hastings Road and Lower Gravel Road, Bromley

In 1917 Bromley Council approved plans by the LGOC to build a garage 'to accommodate the numerous vehicles now required in that southern suburb owing to the growth in bus traffic'. Work did not actually begin until 1923, with the garage opening in April 1924. It had cost £23,000 and was designed to house 60 buses, though the intention was that it would ultimately be enlarged to hold 100.

The garage was one of three allocated for use by Thomas Tilling under an agreement with the LGOC over the former's permitted share of London bus traffic. Thus Tilling's own design of petrol-electric was used in the earliest days, and it was not until 1949 that the last ex-Tilling petrol STLs were replaced — in the short term by 17 hired Leeds City Transport Roe-bodied diesel-engined AEC Regents of 1934. These worked from November 1949 to June 1950 and then went for scrap. Mechanically they were similar to the standard STL, with fluid flywheels and preselector gearboxes.

The first RTs appeared in 1948, with the last departing some 30 years later; RFs appeared in 1952 to replace single-deck LTs on the 227, a busy route which then required 26 single-deckers. Long rear-engined single-deckers eventually ousted the RFs, with MBs arriving in 1968 and SMSs in 1971, followed by DMSs in 1972. The garage also worked one of the first four

minibus routes introduced at the behest of the GLC, initially with FS-type Ford Transit/Strachans minibuses. These were replaced in 1976 by BSs (ECW-bodied Bristol LHSs), and then in 1978 by the longer BL (LH/ECW) type. RMs were fairly late on the scene, first appearing in 1975, and were replaced by Ts in 1984. LSs replaced SMSs in 1977, and the BLs left in 1985. From October 1986 all routes were one-person-operated with a fleet of LS and T types.

One notable allocation was of prototype Titan B15.005, but this appeared not in the halcyon days of the 1970s but in February 1993. Numbered T1131, it was leased from Ensign, and was subsequently sold to Blue Triangle.

Like most garages, the allocation had included various types of single-decker, but it went from 1984 until 1997 without seeing any new double-deckers; then, under Stagecoach ownership, Northern Counties-bodied Volvo Olympians of the VN class arrived, soon followed by Alexander-bodied VA-class Olympians.

To mark the 75th anniversary of the garage, RM613 worked several of its routes on 29 August 1999. The 2001 fleet at Bromley is very modern, with most of the recent Olympians having moved on, though nine are required for school routes, including two on contract to Surrey County Council. Double-deck route 194 needs seven low-floor Dennis Trident/Alexander TAS buses of 10m length, while the 208 has 22 of the longer Trident/Alexander TAs of 10.5m length. Four routes use dual-door Dennis Dart SLF/Alexander ALX200 single-deckers, completing a marked contrast with the position just a few years ago.

Below:
An RM swings hard left as it leaves Bromley garage in 1978. To the right, near another entrance to the garage, is a rather utilitarian bus shelter. *John Gillham*

CATFORD (TL)
Bromley Road, Catford

The LGOC opened its garage in Bromley Road, Catford, in 1914, but this closed in January 1915 when it was requisitioned by the War Department. It was released late in 1920 but handed over to Thomas Tilling, which moved to it the buses and crews from its Lewisham garage, where space was limited: on 23 October that year, 62 petrol-electric buses of type TTA1 went out on four routes from Lewisham in the morning and ran back into Catford at the end of the day. The code letter L moved to the new garage, but in 1924 was changed to TL to avoid confusion with the LGOC's Loughton garage.

Catford garage is actually near Bellingham railway station, and at one time buses carried destination blinds reading 'BELLINGHAM Catford Garage'. There were a number of agreements between the LGOC and Tilling over the years, and a new one in 1923 doubled the size of fleet operated by Tilling in London. To cater for this, the LGOC proposed to build new garages at Bromley and Sidcup. Tilling did not wish to accept Sidcup garage, so Catford was considerably enlarged instead. Further work at Catford took place when the roof was raised in the early 1930s for covered-top double-deckers and again to make ready for RTs in 1948; second time round the cost was a modest £620. The garage was again modernised in 1970.

By June 1939 the garage was operating a mix of STs and STLs — all petrol-engined and many of them former Tilling vehicles, including open-stair STs. All told, its maximum scheduled requirement was for 89 STs and 77 STLs. During the war some 77 of the buses allocated were parked overnight at three different dispersal sites — actually various nearby roads. That total was about half of the garage's fleet. Later in the war, a maximum of 31 ex-LGOC STs towing producer-gas trailers were allocated to the garage; staff had to be specially trained in their operation, and they were confined to routes without any appreciable gradients.

By July 1954 the garage had an allocation of no fewer than 194 RTs — far more than any other garage in the fleet (though it was one of the largest garages and in early 1954 had a scheduled requirement for 189 buses, ousting Upton Park to become the largest in the fleet). RTs remained in large numbers until the late 1960s and did not disappear altogether until 1978. RMs appeared in 1968, but by the mid-1970s DMSs formed a big part of the fleet, with over 80 being eventually allocated; from mid-1983 they were replaced by Ts. The garage had been the first to be allocated SMs, in January 1970, and SMSs followed in 1971; both went in 1976, to be replaced by SMDs for a couple of years, and eventually a few LSs arrived in 1984. In late 1989 Catford also became the first garage to receive MWs — Wright-bodied Mercedes-Benz midibuses.

In 1984, 'summer' weather permitting, the garage operated an open-top Fleetline (DM948) on a special service from Greenwich to the Thames Barrier, a second open-topper (DM1102) being added later. A trial on part of route 180 for a few days in August 1992 saw operation of an air-conditioned six-wheel Volvo Olympian destined for Hong Kong.

In the early days of tendering the garage did considerably better than most, with (in 1994) a requirement for 104 double-deckers and 18 single-deckers — totals very similar to those of mid-2001. But the fleet has changed considerably with, for example, all 78 Ts gone. In their place are a large number of Northern Counties-bodied Volvo Olympians (VNs) plus 32 low-floor Dennis Trident/Alexanders (a mix of

Below:
The crowded forecourt at Catford, with Fleetlines and Routemasters, emphasises the fact that the garage has a large allocation. The Routemaster on the 180 and the Fleetline just visible ahead of it are queueing to enter the garage proper. *Kevin Lane*

long TAs and shorter TASs). Single-deckers include 35 Dennis Darts (25 of them low-floor SLDs with Alexander bodies) and seven Mercedes-Benz Varios with Plaxton Beaver 2 29-seat bodies (MBs).

ORPINGTON (OB)
Unit 17 (later Unit 5), Nugent Trading Estate,
off Cray Avenue, St Mary Cray

Orpington Buses was set up in August 1986 as a separate operation under the wing of London Buses. It passed to the Selkent subsidiary and then finally to Stagecoach Selkent. It closed in December 1995 following the loss of most Orpington-area routes to CentreWest.

It used the trading name 'Roundabout', and routes were numbered with an 'R' prefix. It began with routes R1 to R6, and at the close was working routes R1 to R4, plus R8 and R11. The original fleet consisted of 24 Iveco Daily/Robin Hood 21-seaters plus nine VW LT55/Optare CityPacers. Subsequently various other types and sizes were added, including 13 MCW Metroriders seating between 28 and 33 in 1988, five 33-seat Carlyle-bodied Mercedes-Benz 811Ds in 1989 and 15 Dennis Darts with Carlyle bodies in 1990. One final batch of buses came in 1993 in the form of 10 Iveco Daily/Marshall 23-seaters.

PLUMSTEAD (PD)
Plumstead Road, opposite Plumstead railway station

Originally intended to be called Thamesmead, Plumstead garage is well sited to serve the growing Thamesmead area. The GLC had approved the construction of the new garage, with a capacity of up to 180 buses, to replace Abbey Wood and the existing Plumstead garages. The garage cost nearly £6 million, and part of the site was previously within the precincts of Woolwich Arsenal, though no explosives were found during construction! The garage stands on a 4.7-acre plot of land on an island site within a circulatory road layout north of Plumstead Road and has room for 135 buses under cover. The garage is of brick with a steel framework, while the office block, including stores, staff facilities and a restaurant, has a reinforced concrete frame.

On its opening in October 1981 Plumstead was an all-MD depot, with an initial requirement for a maximum of 81 scheduled buses. From September 1982 new Titans were allocated, ultimately replacing all the MDs by late June 1983: a ceremonial last MD was driven on route 122 back to the garage by Dr David Quarmby, Managing Director of London Buses, as part of LT's 50th anniversary celebrations. By June 1983 the garage was all-Titan, but from March 1986 Olympians began arriving in quantity to replace the type.

The garage began by operating 11 routes, two of which were new, while the others came from the two garages that were replaced. But the 1981 scheduled requirement for 81 buses compares with a 2001 total of 159, so, unlike many, the garage is today running not far short of total capacity. By far the biggest requirement is for route 53, a route not even worked by Plumstead in its earliest days; now it needs 49 TAs (low-floor 10.5m Dennis Tridents with Alexander ALX400 bodies), while three more routes (96, 122 and 472) employ a further 42 of the type. Other double-deck routes still require some 30 Volvo Olympians with Northern Counties bodies. Single-deckers are a mix of 12 step-entrance Dennis Darts and 18 low-floor examples. Finally, there are also eight Mercedes-Benz Varios with Plaxton Beaver 29-seat bodies for route 380.

THE ORIGINAL LONDON SIGHTSEEING TOUR

Above:
An RT deputising for an RM is the most prominent vehicle in this 1977 view of Wandsworth, then still an ordinary operating garage. *Malcolm Scoular*

London Coaches was the first of London's companies to be sold, in May 1992 — over two years ahead of the rest. It was subsequently acquired by the Pullmans Group, which later sold the sightseeing operation to Arriva plc. Since 1999 the company has been known as The Original London Sightseeing Tour.

WANDSWORTH (WD)
Jews Row, Wandsworth

The origins of this garage go back to horse-tram days — 1883, when the South London Tramways Company opened a route to Wandsworth. The company was taken over by the LCC in 1902 and the depot was reconstructed and extended for electric tramcars, the new service beginning in August 1906. Conversion to trolleybus operation began in September 1937 but took rather longer than expected, and the depot went on to run trams and trolleybuses side-by-side for 13 years, until September 1950.

The 1937 changes had seen tram route 12 lose its southern half between Wandsworth and Tooting Junction to new trolleybus route 612. World War 2 intervened before the rest of Wandsworth's trams could be replaced. In the original, revived tram-replacement plans of the early postwar years there was no intention to replace the trolleybuses, and Wandsworth might have become a joint motor-bus/trolleybus depot. But the plan changed, and all trams were replaced at the end of September

1950, with tram route 44 and trolleybus route 612 replaced by new bus route 44. At the same time the depot lost its allocations on two other trolleybus routes. The 35 trams and 21 trolleybuses were replaced by 75 RTs, though within months RTLs replaced the RTs.

RMs arrived at the garage in 1970, but it was in 1975, with the allocation of DMs, that the last RTs ran; they had replaced RTLs in 1967. The DMs lasted till 1980, when RMs replaced them. DMSs had appeared in 1971 for one-person operation, but Metrobuses replaced them from late 1983.

The garage closed in July 1987, its duties being taken over by Putney and Victoria, but an instance of how complicated it was all becoming is given by route 22: previously worked by Wandsworth and Clapton, it moved to Putney and Ash Grove.

In the winter of 1987 Wandsworth was used for storing those London Coaches vehicles for which there was no room at Battersea. Then in April 1988 it reopened, with the London Coaches coaching fleet and Round London Sightseeing Tour vehicles all moving in. Oddly enough, this was not the garage's first connection with London sightseeing, since back in summer 1972 it had provided spare conductors to work on the East Kent open-top, open-rear-platform Guy Arabs on the Round London Sightseeing Tour that was operated on LT's behalf by Samuelsons. In November 1997 London Coaches' owner Pullmans Group sold the sightseeing operation, along with Wandsworth garage and all but one of the double-deckers, to Arriva.

—④—

Non-London Buses operators of LT routes

A minor but nevertheless significant part in current London bus operations is played by a number of small and not-so-small operators. In the early days of tendering, National Bus Company or former NBC concerns such as Eastern National and London Country did well. Some of the more successful medium-sized or smaller operators were later taken over; for example, Metrobus became part of Go-Ahead Group, which already had a big share in London operations. Some of the newcomers faded from the scene quite quickly, a few of those which had previously run only coaches finding that running buses every day for long periods was a more demanding task than expected. Others have been more successful.

Many of the operators run from fairly basic yards or depots that cannot really be described as garages. A parking area, a bus-washing machine and a portable building or two represent the sum total in many cases, and can certainly not be described as photogenic.

This chapter records most of the sites that have been used or are still in use since route-tendering began. It is set out alphabetically by operator. However, the listing does not go into great detail on the various complicated tendering operations of London Country and its successors; it would require a separate book to explain these. Included, however, are larger operators which were not involved in the sale of the London Buses subsidiaries.

AirLinks
(formerly Speedlink Airport Services)

Since March 1999 this operator has run five air-conditioned Dennis Dart SLF / Plaxton Pointer 2s on the H30 'Airport Connect' free service, a joint LT Buses/ British Airports Authority initiative. It has two bases at Heathrow, at Building 471, Northwood Road, and at the West Ramp, both at Heathrow North, but the H30 buses are operated from 682 Arndale Road, Feltham.

Armchair

Since 1999 Armchair has moved into a larger depot at the end of Commerce Way, Brentford, but also still parks some vehicles on its original site in the road. Tendered work began in 1990 and has since built up, with double-deckers and single-deckers operated mainly in the Ealing, Hounslow and Richmond areas.

Arriva Croydon & North Surrey
(formerly London & Country)

From June 1998 this company, previously part of London & Country, became responsible for Leatherhead garage, as well as bases at Hounslow, Merstham and Beddington Farm, Croydon. A new contract for route 85 (Kingston–Putney) saw 13 DAF DB250 chassis with Northern Counties Palatine II bodies enter service on the route in May 1998, operated from Leatherhead garage. However, sudden termination of the lease saw the route moved to operate from the forecourt of London United's Fulwell garage for some months in 1999 until London United took it over later in the year, along with 12 of the buses.

Arriva East Herts & Essex
(formerly County Bus & Coach)

County Bus won its first London work with effect from August 1990 with routes 66 (Romford–Leytonstone) and 103 (North Romford–Hornchurch), and duly built up its portfolio, although the 103 and its leased Leyland Olympians were passed to Grey-Green in January 1991.

County had been owned by Lynton Travel, which was taken over by West Midlands Travel in 1994. In 1996 WMT sold the business on to Cowie, which placed the company under management of Leaside Buses. In September 1997 the Edmonton depot was moved from premises in Gibbs Road to the former MTL/London Suburban base at Edmonton Wharf, Lea Valley Trading Estate (later transfered to Arriva London North). By 2001 the company was running some six tendered routes.

Arriva Kent Thameside

Despite the transfer of many of its routes to Arriva's 'red' subsidiaries, the former Kentish Bus still operates about 50 buses in South East London from bases at Dartford and Northfleet. The latter is the only surviving former Country Area garage built by the LPTB.

Arriva The Shires

The Shires has a small number of tendered services in the Harrow and Watford areas, of which route 142

(Brent Cross–Watford) probably holds a record for having been operated continuously for several years.

Blue Triangle

Although based somewhat remotely at Unit 3C, Denver Trading Estate, Ferry Lane, Rainham, Essex, Blue Triangle is well known on the London scene for helping out other operators with staffing problems. An example was the operation of part of route 60 (Old Coulsdon–Streatham) for Capital Logistics and more recently Central London service C10 for Limebourne. The first LT tendered route, in 1999, was the new 474 (Canning Town–East Beckton District Centre), worked with nine new East Lancs Lolyne-bodied Dennis Tridents. Since then, two more routes have been gained.

Boro'line Maidstone

In the late 1980s the Maidstone municipal operation built up a big tendered operation of London services before collapsing with financial problems. In the spring of 1992 Proudmutual, owner of Kentish Bus, bought Boro'line's London operation and use of Crayford depot (rented from the London Borough of Bexley) along with 55 buses and 145 staff for a reported £300,000, making Kentish Bus then the largest operator of tendered London routes.

BTS

BTS of Borehamwood gained route 292 after the previous operator ran into difficulties. It added a further route (114) in January 1991, and in 1993 improved its base in Station Road, Borehamwood, with a new workshop with capacity for eight buses. From December the company lost the 292 but gained the 13, operated with RMLs leased from LT. BTS subsequently sold out to Sovereign, owned by Blazefield Holdings. Its operations were duly renamed London Sovereign, and ultimately the Borehamwood base was closed and the routes moved to Edgware, where Sovereign shares the garage with Metroline.

Capital Logistics

Work for LT began in August 1993 with a contract for a new route H26 (Sparrow Farm–Hatton Cross), for which Mercedes-Benz 709Ds with Plaxton bodies and wheelchair lifts were bought. The route was run from an outstation at the Flightpath car park, off Eastern Perimeter Road, Heathrow, the main base being in Sipson Road, West Drayton. A notable acquisition was the fleet of Ikarus-bodied DAF SB220s for the 726 when this route was taken over from London Coaches (Kent) in April 1998. For a time the Harris Bus depot at Belvedere was used as an outstation, then the Bexley Council depot in Crayford, and later still the Southlands Coaches base in the former London Country garage at Swanley; following this the route was worked entirely from West Drayton, before the Bexley Council depot was again used as an outstation.

Less successful was the winning of the contract for route 60 from September 1998, which was sub-contracted out, initially to Stagecoach Selkent for a time, before being worked by a variety of operators. Ultimately a base was set up at a coach and lorry park at Commerce Way (off Purley Way), Croydon, and buses for the 726 were also worked from here in 1999. In June 1999 the company was taken over by Tellings-Golden Miller, which continued to run the LT routes but later passed the 60 to Arriva.

Connex Bus

This relatively new operator won Central London routes 3 and N3 from February 2000, operating these with a fleet of Dennis Tridents with Alexander ALX400 bodies, and has since won several more LT/TfL tenders. It is based at Unit 10, Beddington Cross, Croydon, Surrey and has another yard nearby. In mid-2001 the buses and operations of Limebourne were acquired, with the latter's base in Silverthorne Way continuing in use.

Crystals

This operator has specialised in accessible minibus work but was an early LT contract operator, winning route 146 with Mercedes-Benz 608Ds in 1985. Later, HTI Maxeta-bodied Leyland Cubs worked the service from the company's Orpington depot. Currently two Orpington-area routes, R2 and R7, are worked by Mercedes-Benz 709Ds and 811Ds with the operator's own bodywork; they operate from a base at 127 Dartford Road, Crayford, Kent. From there the company also uses two Mercedes-Benz Vario / Plaxton Beaver 2 midibuses on route B14, plus a number of other vehicles on LT Mobility work from the same base; the fleet for this includes two Optare Solos.

Docklands Transit

Harry Blundred, best known for introducing minibuses successfully at Devon General, began running minibuses in London Docklands in March 1989 from a base at Silvertown. Initially, operation was of services gained via the Metropolitan Traffic Commissioner and without LT approval, which meant that Travelcards and the London Boroughs' funded scheme for pensioners' travel were not available and revenue was low. The operation was closed in November 1990.

Subsequently, in March 1993, Docklands Transit won three routes in East London, operated with Mercedes-Benz midibuses, later adding route 106 (Finsbury Park–Whitechapel), which was worked with 18 Dennis Dart/Plaxtons. These operated from the Silvertown premises, which had been retained. In July 1997 the operation, with 18 Darts and 21 Mercedes-Benz 811Ds, was bought by Stagecoach Holdings and absorbed into Stagecoach East London.

Durham Travel Services (trading as London Easylink)

A well-established and successful County Durham coach operator, DTS began running route 185 (Victoria–Lewisham) from February 2001 with 20 Volvo B7TL double-deckers with Plaxton President bodies. Servicing is contracted to Volvo, but the buses are based at the secure Transco gas site at 709 Old Kent Road, London SE15. The site has fuelling and washing facilities, the drive-through washing machine being of a special design which automatically shuts down and drains the system when the air temperature nears freezing point.

Eastern National

Unusual Wadham Stringer-bodied Bedford YMQ/S midibuses were used by Eastern National when it took over route W9 (Enfield–Muswell Hill) in July 1985. Buses were outstationed at an Enfield base at Carter-hatch, worked as an outstation of Brentwood garage. That garage worked directly the 195, taken over on the same date, initially with Bristol VRs, later Ford Transits and eventually Mercedes-Benz midibuses. With further routes won, a Walthamstow base was opened at Lowhall Lane, but serious staff shortages saw routes being run by staff from Braintree, Basildon and Southend.

Early in 1987 Walthamstow and a base at Ponders End were providing buses for some six routes. Those worked from Walthamstow were subsequently lost to Grey-Green on retendering, while in 1990 Eastern National was divided, with all the London tendered routes passing to sister company Thamesway.

Ensignbus/Capital Citybus

This was one of the earliest operators of tendered services and has subsequently been one of the most successful. It began with route 145 (Redbridge-Dagenham) in June 1986 and over the next few years went on building up operations using former London Fleetlines worked from Purfleet. In mid-1989 it took over East Midland's Frontrunner operation, adding three more routes to its portfolio, and this was followed in November 1989 by the opening of a new depot at Dagenham Dock. It was not all gains as the original route, the 145, was lost to East London in 1991. But the *débâcle* of London Forest in autumn 1991 gave the company six extra routes to run at relatively short notice.

In January 1991 Ensign's LT operations had been taken over by the CNT group, holding company of Hong Kong-based Citybus, and this led to a number of new buses' gaining 'lucky' registration numbers such as 888; the 'new' company (actually the previously dormant Frontrunner) was eventually renamed Capital Citybus.

Below:
The main Dagenham Dock depot of what is now First Capital has been in use for the growing fleet since 1989; this view was taken in 1992. *Alan Millar*

Above:
Headroom in First Capital's Northumberland Park maintenance building is sufficient to permit jacks (rather than pits) to be used in servicing double-deckers. *Alan Millar*

Below:
First Capital's base at Waterden Road, Hackney, came into use in 1996, initially with an allocation of 45 buses. *Author*

An offshoot (legally Walthamstow Citybus) was established to run North London operations, with vehicles and services being based at Northumberland Park (near the Underground's Victoria Line depot), and in 1992 this gained two more former London Forest routes that had been temporarily covered by other operators. Various other routes followed, and more recently the continued expansion has resulted in the opening of an outstation to Dagenham nearby at Choats Road.

The sudden expansion brought a huge demand for more buses, and it was said that, at Dagenham Dock on a Sunday, Atlanteans, VRs, Dominators, Fleetlines, Metrobuses and even an RM could be seen together. But new buses were being bought too, including some of the last Workington-built Leyland Olympians, with Northern Counties Palatine bodies. Yet another depot is at Waterden Road, Hackney, opened in 1996.

A management buy-out in December 1995 brought the company back into UK ownership, and in 1998 it was purchased by FirstGroup, becoming 'First Capital'. Subsequently a depot at Morson Road, Ponder's End, previously used by Thamesway for LT work, has also been passed within FirstGroup to First Capital, together with its buses and staff.

Epsom Buses

This old-established coach operator began bus work on a commercial basis for Surrey County Council in 1986 but did not undertake any London operations until October 1997, when it took over two former London General routes (S1 and 413) which were reassigned. It has since won a number of further routes, all worked by a mix of Dennis Darts (some low-floor) and Mercedes-Benz Varios. All work from Blenheim Road, Epsom.

Frontrunner South East

The Frontrunner company was set up by East Midland in the early days of the deregulation outside London. The aim was to diversify, to guard against possible crippling competition on East Midland's home ground, and Frontrunner won two London services from September 1988 in the London area as well as some Essex County Council contracts. Stagecoach bought East Midland in 1989 and sold the Frontrunner operation to Ensignbus in June of that year.

Grey-Green

Grey-Green had been Cowie's first venture into public transport, having been acquired 'by accident' in 1980. At the time, Cowie was buying the parent George Ewer Group for its motor-trade interests rather than for its Grey-Green coaches (and, later, buses). It then discovered that running buses was more profitable.

Grey-Green began with just one tendered bus route, the 173, worked by secondhand former Greater Manchester Fleetlines based at a depot on a trading estate in Oxlow Lane, Dagenham, operated by its Dix Coaches subsidiary. It soon built up more bus work, with a

Below:
It was Grey-Green's success with London bus work which brought about Cowie Group's enthusiasm for buses and ultimately led to the Arriva of today. This was Grey-Green's old-established Stamford Hill base, for very many years just a coach depot. *Alan Millar*

'plum' in the shape of high-profile Central London route 24, won in November 1988 and worked from its Stamford Hill base. When Grey-Green bought from Simco 314 the former County operation on route 103, together with its Leyland Olympians, the latter operated from Dagenham depot on weekdays and Stamford Hill on Sundays. As the number of tendered routes increased, buses at Barking and Stamford Hill were working some 14 LRT routes. The Barking depot was in Ripple Road, where modern servicing and repair facilities had been built.

Ultimately Grey-Green was to give up its coach operations, concentrating entirely on buses, and when the Cowie group restyled itself as Arriva, the Grey-Green company was renamed Arriva London North East. The garage at High Road, Stamford Hill, closed in March 1998, with operations moving to the one-time trolleybus depot (later bus garage) in Rookwood Road, Stamford Hill.

Hackney Community Transport (trading as CT Plus)

This relative newcomer to London bus operations began in June 1999 with Mobility Bus work in North and East London from its depot at Hertford Road, London N1. Subsequently, in 2001, it won a tender for a mainstream route, the 153, with a fleet of Dennis Dart SLFs with Caetano Nimbus bodies. Both types are now based at the yard of Ash Grove garage (otherwise operated by East Thames Buses) but return to Hertford Road for maintenance.

Harris Bus

Harris Bus had begun expanding bus operation in Essex from deregulation day in 1986 but did not win its first London contract (for a schooldays-only route) until well into the 1990s. Then in 1997/8 it won six routes, all to be worked by new buses, mainly double-deckers, except for the cross-river 108, worked with Optare Excels. It had three routes north of the river and two south, working them partly from its base at Manor Road, West Thurrock, Grays, and from the Acorn Industrial Estate, Dartford Road, Crayford. The latter was later replaced by a new depot at Crabtree Manor Way North, Belvedere, which opened in February 1998.

Unfortunately the whole operation ran into difficulties and went into administrative receivership in December 1999. London Transport Buses took over the running on a temporary basis and then made a full takeover in 2000, continuing to use the Belvedere base but centring operations on its own Ash Grove garage, which was reopened.

Javelin Coaches

This Battersea-based operation took over the running of nine Mobility Bus routes in 1992. The buses and work were later acquired by F. E. Thorpe.

Limebourne

Limebourne Travel was originally part of the Q-Drive group and had built up operations from Silverthorne Road, London SW11, with operation of four tendered routes. But in November 1998 the group went into receivership, and the existing fleet was reposessed. However, a successful management buy-out under the name of Independent Way enabled the operations to continue. After a period of hiring, some secondhand Dennis Darts were acquired and more new ones ordered for operation of five routes, plus another under sub-contract.

In August 2000 the company bought the London operations and vehicles of Travel London after the latter failed to get planning approval to continue to use its base in Stewarts Lane. The buses and two routes continued to be operated by Limebourne. However, in 2001 reliability problems led to one route being taken on by Blue Triangle, and then the whole business was taken over by Connex Bus, which continued using the Silverthorne Road base, shared with a coach company.

London Buslines

Len Wright Travel was based in Worton Road, Isleworth, and in 1985 won one of the first London routes to be put out to tender, the 81 (Hounslow–Slough), using former DM Fleetlines that had been new to LT. Two years later, new Leyland Lynxes were acquired for the route. Over a period of several years the business went on to win a number of London routes, though some were lost on retendering. The business subsequently became a part of Q-Drive.

Later contracts saw further new buses acquired, including Leyland Olympians with Alexander or Northern Counties bodies and Mercedes-Benz 709D and 811D models. A base was established at Greenford, and in November 1997 Isleworth was closed and its work moved to Southall. A year earlier, CentreWest had taken over all Q-Drive's service-bus operations, including Bee Line in Slough and Bracknell. Following the takeover, two routes newly won by London Buslines were both taken on by CentreWest. In mid-2001 CentreWest merged the remaining London Buslines operations and staff into its own organisation, and the base at Middlesex Business Park, Bridge Road, Southall, was vacated. Just one route had not been acquired with the 1996 takeover — the C10 (Victoria–Elephant & Castle) — and that was assigned to Q-Drive's coach-operating subsidiary, Limebourne Travel.

London Cityrama

This operation began by running sightseeing buses in London, mainly using former LT Daimler Fleetline double-deckers. In March 1986 it started operating route 200 (Streatham Hill–Raynes Park) using 11 former London DMSs and in February 1987 also gained the 196 (Norwood Junction–Brixton–Islington)

Below:
The base at Southall used by London Buslines both before and after its acquisition by CentreWest closed in August 2001. The bus washer is prominent in this view. *Author*

using former South Yorkshire PTE Fleetlines. The vehicles were based at Queenstown Road, Battersea. The 200 contract was relinquished in December 1988 and the 196 in October 1989, both being taken over by other operators at short notice.

London Country Bus Services

Starting in July 1985, some 10 routes were won before the company was split into four in September 1986. Among the garages involved were Chelsham, Dorking, Godstone, Garston and Hatfield. In addition, route 268 (Golders Green–Finchley Road) was worked from Scratchwood Service Station on the M1, as an outstation to Garston.

London Country North East

Apart from one route worked by St Albans garage, this company did not figure significantly in the LT tendering system. It was later split to form Sovereign and County, both of which were rather more successful.

London Country North West/ Luton & District

Two notable contracts won in 1987 were for route C2 (Regent's Park–Parliament Hill Fields) and 153 (Archway–Islington), both of which were run from a new base at the NFC's Pickfords depot at Coppetts Road, Muswell Hill. Both were relinquished after the company was given notice to quit the base in June 1988.

Other routes were operated from Garston garage without problems.

London Country South East/ Kentish Bus

This operator won by far the largest number of LT tendered routes, building up steadily in earlier days and then greatly increasing its share of work after it acquired the LT routes and buses previously operated by Boro'line Maidstone.

One of the earliest routes was the 42 (Aldgate–Camberwell Green), worked from February 1987 with

Above:
For some years London Country and most of its successors ran extensive tendered operations in London. When Beddington Farm, Croydon, depot opened, it had been planned to close Chelsham and Godstone garages, but Godstone (seen here) was temporarily reprieved to run route 196 when London Cityrama relinquished it at short notice. Some of the Atlanteans for the 196 are parked outside, on a Sunday. *Author*

Leyland Nationals based initially at the Catford National Express depot and later at the former Samuelson garage at Victoria. Later route P4 was also similarly moved.

Routes won at the time the Bexleybus operation was set up included the 51 (Orpington/Green Street Green–Woolwich), which necessitated reopening Swanley garage as an outstation just eight months after it had been closed.

Three routes running into Central London won from January 1990 were the 22A (Clapham Park–London Bridge), 22B (Homerton Hospital–Piccadilly) and 55 (Clapham–Tottenham Court Road) — all based at a British Road Services depot in Leyton, which was also responsible for fuelling, cleaning and maintenance. Some 50 buses were said to be involved, and the deal with BRS was publicised as a £1 million-a-year five-year contract.

Another noteworthy win was of the Routemaster-operated route 19 from April 1993. Initially it was operated from a base in the New Covent Garden Market, where cleaning, fuelling and light maintenance could be undertaken, but in October the base was moved to land next to the former LT bus garage in Hester Road, Battersea. Also in October 1993 the former Boro'line Maidstone base at Crayford was vacated, with the buses being moved to Dartford garage. The same month witnessed the acquisition of the buses and services of Transcity, Sidcup, including operations on LT routes 286 and B15.

Early 1994 saw Kentish Bus take over eight routes in the Lewisham area, for which it ordered 65 new buses, bringing its London fleet up to nearly two-thirds of its total operation. However, by 1995 it was beginning to encounter operational problems, and, at the end of the year or in the following January, four routes that had been worked from a base in Lewisham passed to Metrobus of Orpington, together with a number of vehicles.

Another transfer of a different kind was the move of the Leyton-based buses, together with some other routes in East London, to the former LT garage at Ash Grove, though Kentish Bus always called it Cambridge Heath. Then, in February 1998, Ash Grove was vacated, with work transferring to Cowie Leaside. The Olympians on route 242 moved to Clapton, while those on the 176 and 188 were moved to Norwood to replace unpopular Volvo Citybuses.

London Country South West, later London & Country

When route 110 (Twickenham–Cranford) was taken on from January 1987 it used former Greater Manchester PTE Leyland Atlanteans based at Addlestone garage, these being the first double-deckers allocated there since 1972. Various other routes were subsequently won covering a wide area of South London, such as 85 (Putney Bridge–Kingston) and 176 (Penge–Oxford Circus), and a number in the Croydon area. The closure of Chelsham garage was cancelled after the 196 was taken over at short notice when Cityrama gave it up, but the route was subsequently transferred to London General.

The growing number of London routes led to the reopening of the former LT garage at Walworth, with two routes formerly operated from Newington Butts being based there from January 1993, along with newly acquired Peckham-area route P3. A short-lived operation on route 105 (Heathrow–Greenford) began in April 1996 using new low-floor Dennis Darts worked from a base at Kelvin Industrial Estate, Greenford; within seven months the route and buses had been reassigned to CentreWest.

Londonlinks

British Bus set up this operation early in 1995 to manage most of London & Country's London contract work. It came under the overall control of Kentish Bus at Northfleet and took over all the LT services operated out of Beddington Farm (Croydon), Dunton Green and Walworth depots. It was to be a short-lived operation, however, for at the end of August 1997 all Londonlinks' Croydon work, including 94 buses, was transferred to London & Country control, while Walworth garage closed on the same date.

London Suburban Bus

A new London operation of Gemsam Holdings, which ran in Liverpool under the Liverbus fleetname, won contracts for two London routes — 4 (Archway Station–Waterloo Station) and 271 (Liverpool Street Station–Highgate Village) — from September 1993. Soon afterwards a third contract was won, for the busy route 41 (Archway–Tottenham Hale). The company operated from a base at the Hastingwood (Lea Valley) Trading Estate, with space for some 50 buses.

In April 1995 MTL Trust Holdings, owner of London Northern, acquired the whole of Gemsam for £2 million and in November absorbed London Suburban into London Northern. In 1996 the contract for the 41 transferred to Cowie Leaside and the Edmonton base closed in June. It was later reopened by another London operater.

Metrobus

This was one of the most successful operators of LT tendered routes, gaining a reputation for a high standard of service. It won its first tender, for the 61 (Bromley North–Chislehurst) and associated 361 (Bromley North–Green Street Green) in August 1986 and followed this up with a steady increase in the amount of tendered work, as well as developing its own commercial services.

All operations have been worked from a former farm at Farnborough Hill, Green Street Green, near Orpington. The depot has been steadily improved over the years.

The company was bought by Go-Ahead Group in September 1999 for £14 million, this including other operations based at Godstone and Lewes.

What is now Metropolitan Omnibus began London work with Metrobuses on school workings, but in 1999 won two all-day routes with new Volvo/East Lancs single-deckers. This is the depot in Harlesden. *David Wyatt*

Metropolitan Omnibus (formerly London Traveller)

Operations for LT were initially limited to a number of schooldays-only services worked by Metrobuses. But in the summer of 1999 the company won its first contracts for all-day routes — the 187 and 487 — and bought 15 Volvo B6BLE/East Lancs Spryte single-deckers; five more arrived in 2000 after route 187 was extended.

Originally the company had a base at Great Central Way, Neasden, but this was given up and it moved to the former Scancoaches depot in Goodhall Street, off Old Oak Common Lane, Harlesden. Five schooldays-only LT routes were also operated in 2001.

Mitcham Belle

This well-established coach operator began its bus operations with a fleet of 12 Dennis Dart SLF/Plaxton Pointer 2 buses bought for route 127 (Purley–Tooting), which the company took over in April 1999. Two more routes followed in 2000, needing 24 more similar but shorter buses, while a fourth route was won in 2001.

The original coach base at 223 Streatham Road, Mitcham, was barely large enough, and subsequently buses were moved to the DETR depot near Beddington Lane, Croydon; workshops are situated nearby.

Pan Atlas (fleetname 'Atlas Bus')

This Acton-based coach operator won route 112 from July 1988, using Leyland Lynxes, and route 107 with Olympians the following year. In 1994 it lost both on retendering, but Pullmans Ltd, which owned London Coaches, took it over and moved newly-won route 52 with its Leyland Titans to the Atlas base at Atlas Road, near Willesden Junction. Then in November 1994 Metroline acquired Atlas Bus & Coach from the Pullmans Group, continuing it under the Atlas name until September 1996. A year previously, however, the route had been moved back to Willesden garage.

R&I Tours

Already a small coach/minibus operator, this company took over route H2 (Golders Green–Hampstead Garden Suburb) in mid-June 1989, initially using hired minibuses from London Country North West. Tendered operation of the 268 (Golders Green–Finchley Road) had started a week earlier. R&I later gained other routes, including the C11 and C12, operated with larger single-deckers. All told it had five routes, plus a Sunday service on a sixth, when taken over by MTL Trust Holdings in a £2 million deal in October 1995. Also acquired were bases at North Acton and Park Royal.

Sampson's

Coach company Sampson's of Hoddesdon began London bus operation in May 1986 with seven former LT Fleetlines on route 217B (Enfield–Upshire), at the same time gaining two other former LT routes under Essex County Council tender. Reliability problems led to the loss of the Enfield–Upshire route (by now renumbered 317) in June 1988.

Scancoaches

One of the earlier operators of a contracted route, this operator already had a fleet of Scania coaches. For route 283 (West Brompton–Hammersmith Hospital/Willesden Junction) it bought five Scania K92 chassis with Jonckheere dual-door bodies seating 47 with room for 22 standees. These 12m-long buses were unique to the London scene and operated from new premises at Old Oak Lane, Willesden. The tender was lost in July 1989, London United taking over the route, initially with Leyland Nationals and then with Leyland Lynxes.

Sovereign

In December 1990 Sovereign Bus & Coach won tenders for four local services in Harrow, for which it set up a subsidiary company, Sovereign (Harrow). These original routes were retained on re-tender, and additional routes were won in 1999, with the buses being garaged at the Pinner Road, Harrow, garage of Venture Coaches. In 1999 the maintenance facilities there were moved to the former LT garage at Edgware, part of which was now occupied by Sovereign, which has been reformed as Sovereign Buses (London).

Tellings-Golden Miller

For a time, Tellings-Golden Miller was a subsidiary of Midland Fox, and won tenders to operate routes 116 and 117 from August 1991 with secondhand Leyland Nationals provided by that concern. They were fuelled and cleaned at the former London Country Staines garage, though parked outside, with any heavier work being carried out at TGM's coach depot at Byfleet. Problems arose, however, and in February 1992 the bus operation was moved and placed under the control of London & Country at its Addlestone garage, from where the buses subsequently ran, initially still in their blue and white colours.

Stephen Telling subsequently reacquired the company, gaining a contract for the S3 (Sutton–Worcester Park) — also partly funded by the London Borough of Sutton — and commencing operation of it in March 1995. From there TGM went on to win an increasing number of London contracts. In June 1999 the Capital Logistics

Below:
The growing business of Tellings-Golden Miller has a base at the rear of Fulwell bus garage, the main part of which is occupied by London United. *Geoff Rixon*

base near Heathrow was taken over with some 170 vehicles (including coaches), plus a base in Commerce Way, Croydon, and four tendered London routes. In July this was followed by acquisition of the Albion Road, Hounslow, base of Arriva Croydon & North Surrey, again with staff, vehicles and six LT routes. A new contract for the 726 (Heathrow–Bromley) was won from April 2000; having taken over Capital Logistics in 1999, TGM was already running this route before being awarded the new contract.

Acquisition of part of the former LT garage at Fulwell gave the company a valuable base near many of its LT operations, leaving mainly the non-London services based at Byfleet.

Thamesway

When Eastern National was divided into two, all its London tendered work passed to Thamesway, which by the end of 1993 was running 10 such routes, almost all worked with minibuses. One of them, the 214 (Parliament Hill Fields–Highgate–Liverpool Street), had a requirement for 17 Dennis Darts and was worked by Ponders End garage. In March 1996 all routes were registered under the name of Essex Buses, which was set up to manage Thamesway and Eastern National and was a subsidiary of FirstBus. In 1998 the 214 was reassigned to MTL London, and, in September that year, 10 routes run from the Ponders End garage were transferred to First Capital, along with 36 Mercedes-Benz midibuses and 14 Dennis Darts. One route, the 193, remained with Thamesway and operated from that time out of a new base at Bryant Avenue, Harold Wood, known as Romford depot. In 1999 staff problems saw part of the 193 allocation move from Romford to Basildon, with several of the Mercedes-Benz midibuses.

F. E. Thorpe & Sons

Operation of the Interstation Carelink service linking main-line stations in London was begun in 1992 with two Mercedes-Benz 709Ds with 14-seat Alexander (Belfast) bodies with wheelchair lifts. These worked from a base at 272 Latimer Road, London W10. In 1996 the service was improved in frequency and size when four Optare Excels (the first in London) were put to work on replacement services SL1 and SL2, now running clockwise and anti-clockwise.

The company also won other tendered services, with

a small service from Putney in 1995, and then the 210 (Finsbury Park–Brent Cross), an old-established service recently operated by Grey-Green. A new depot was opened for this service at Unit 5, Fourth Way, Wembley Stadium Trading Estate, additionally replacing a yard at the GEC Estate, East Lane, North Wembley, from where operations had previously been run. In 2000 the operator won another route in the Acton area, convenient for the new depot. Earlier, in August 1997, the company had also taken over some other Mobility Bus routes from Wandsworth-based Javelin Coaches, together with the four Mercedes-Benz 709D/Wadham Stringer minibuses used.

Transcity Coaches

Route B15 was won under tender in 1991 and was unusual in being operated with three-axle Talbot Pullman midibuses. The following year, a larger route, the 286, was taken on, requiring eight Dennis Darts. The vehicles were based at Sidcup. In late 1993 the buses and services, which included a number of non-London routes, were taken over by Kentish Bus.

Travel London

From June 1998 this National Express subsidiary won two Central London routes, the 211 (Waterloo–Hammersmith) and the C1 (Victoria–Kensington High Street), putting Optare Excels on the 211 and Optare Solos (the first in London) on the C1. They were based at the Stewarts Lane (Battersea) rail depot of sister company Gatwick Express. However, planning permission was subsequently refused for bus use of this site. An appeal was turned down in 2000; the company said it was unable to find alternative premises, and staff and vehicles moved to Limebourne's depot nearby.

Wing's Buses

From November 1999 this coach operator began operating route U7 with three Dennis Dart SLFs with East Lancs Spryte bodies in a striking orange, yellow and red livery. A second route, the H50, was begun in April 2000 with similar buses, but painted in two-tone green with a touch of red; buses are also equipped with an automated public-address system which announces the name of each stop. The buses are now based at North Hyde Gardens, Hayes.

Index

As well as what are best described as 'traditional' London bus garages, these indices also list garages and depots in the London area which are in current use with major operators running TfL-contracted services. In addition to the name of the garage/depot it includes the code used by the operator, though not all operators now use garage codes. However, for internal purposes TfL assigns a code to every location, and this is shown, marked with an asterisk. In a few cases this conflicts with the code the operator has adopted, and in others operators are changing their codes to match those allocated by TfL, as explained on page 3. Where two codes are in use for the same location, both are given.

Garages in alphabetical order of location

Abbey Wood (AW) 9, 13, 21
Acton (AT/AN★) 94
Alperton (ON) 4, 10, 11, 17, 95
Ash Grove (AG) 5, 17, 92, 153
Ash Grove (Hackney Community Transport) (HK★) 150
Athol Street, Poplar (C) 22

Barking, Longbridge Road (BK) 134
Barking, Ripple Road (BA/DX★) 76, 149
Battersea, Hester Road (B) 19, 23, 153
Battersea, Hester Road (London General) (BB) 105
Battersea, Hester Road Yard (BA) 86, 153
Battersea, Silverthorne Road (QB★) 146, 151
Beddington Cross, Croydon (BC) 146
Beddington Farm, Croydon (BF/CN★) 3, 7, 86, 145, 153
Belvedere (BV) 92
Bexleyheath (BX) 100
Bow (BW) 134
Brentford (AH★) 145
Brixton (BN) 86
Bromley (TB) 141
Bull Yard, Peckham (PM) 4, 11, 14, 17, 49

Camberwell (Q) 19, 101
Cambridge Heath (Ash Grove) 153
Carshalton (Sutton) (CN) .13, 24
Catford (TL) 142
Chadwell Heath (CH) 136
Chalk Farm (CF) 25
Chelverton Road, Putney (AF) 107
Chiswick (Stamford Brook) (V) 10, 11, 122
Clapham (CA) 26
Clapton (Hackney) (CT) 76
Clay Hall, Old Ford (CL) 27
Colindale (Hendon) (CE) .12, 28
Cricklewood (W) 10, 19, 24
Croydon, Beddington Cross, Beddington Lane (BC) 146
Croydon, Beddington Farm (BF/CN★) 3, 7, 86, 145, 153
Croydon, Brighton Road (TC) 20, 88
Croydon, Redhouse Road and Beddington Lane (MC★) .154

Dagenham, Chequers Lane (DM) 147
Dagenham, Choats Road (DA) 147
Dalston (D) 7, 13, 20, 29

Edgware (EW) 5, 11, 18, 125
Edgware (BT★) 146
Edmonton (EM) 30
Edmonton Wharf (EM/EC★) 77, 153
Elmers End (ED) 16, 17, 31
Enfield (E) 77

Feltham, Arndale Road 145
Finchley (FY) 32
Forest Gate (G) 33
Fulwell (FW) 5, 113, 145
Fulwell (Stanley Road – TGM) (TF★) 155

Gillingham Street, Victoria (GM) 5, 7, 10, 11, 67
Gillingham Street, Victoria Basement (GB) 67
Green Street Green (MB★) 153
Greenford (G) 96

Hackney (Clapton) (CT) 76
Hackney (H) 13, 33
Hackney (Waterden Road, Stratford) (H) 147
Hammersmith (HB) 12, 34
Hammersmith (Riverside) (R) 10, 11, 12, 55
Hanwell (HL) 36
Hanwell (Southall) (HW) 60
Harlesden, Atlas Road (HR/RI★) 127
Harlesden, Goodhall Street (HN★) 154
Harrow (SO★) 155
Harrow Weald (HD) 127
Heathrow (West Ramp) (HR★) 115, 145
Hendon (AE) 8, 37
Hendon (Colindale) (CE) 28
Highgate (Holloway) (HT) 130
Holloway (J) 37
Holloway (Highgate) (HT) 130
Hornchurch (RD) 4, 38
Hounslow (AV) 3, 8, 15, 115
Hounslow (Isleworth) (IH) 12, 15, 40
Hounslow Heath (WK/HH) 117

Ilford (ID) 12, 40
Isleworth (Hounslow) (IH) 12, 15, 40

Kingston (K) 19, 117, 118

Lea Bridge (Leyton) (LB) 12, 40
Leyton (T) 136
Leyton (Lea Bridge) (LB) 12, 40
Loughton (L) 5, 41

Merton (AL) 14, 105
Middle Row, North Kensington (X) 13, 42
Mortlake (M) 10, 11, 13, 19, 42
Muswell Hill (MH) 21, 44

New Cross (NX) 11, 103
Norbiton (NB) 13, 17, 19, 21, 45
North Acton (NA) 131
North Kensington, Middle Row (X) 13, 42
North Street, Romford (NS) 4, 5, 17, 138
North Wembley (NW) 128
Northumberland Park (NP) 148, 149
Norwood (N) 13, 19, 89
Nunhead (AH) 47

Old Ford, Clay Hall (CL) 27
Old Kent Road (DR★) 147
Old Kent Road (P) 7, 19, 49
Orpington (Green Street Green) (MB★) 153
Orpington (Nugent Ind Estate, St Mary Cray) (OB) 143
Orpington (Faraday Way, St Mary Cray) (Y/OR★) 96

Palmers Green (AD) 79
Peckham, Bull Yard (PM) 4, 11, 14, 17, 49
Peckham, Copeland Road (PM) .104
Peckham, Rye Lane (RL) 12, 58
Plumstead (AM) 13, 51
Plumstead (PD) 13, 143
Poplar (PR) 52
Poplar, Athol Street (C) 22
Potters Bar (PB) 8, 10, 131
Putney, Chelverton Road (AF) 107
Putney Bridge (F) 54

Riverside (Hammersmith) (R) 10, 11, 12, 55
Romford, North Street (NS) 4, 5, 17, 138
Rye Lane, Peckham (RL) 12, 58

St Mary Cray [(Nugent Ind. Estate)], Orpington (OB) . . .143
St Mary Cray (Faraday Way), Orpington (Y/OR★) 96
Seven Kings (AP) 10, 58
Shepherds Bush (S) 17, 119
Sidcup (SP) 12, 59
Southall (Hanwell) (HW) 60
Southall (LW★) 151
Stamford Brook (Chiswick) (V) 10, 11, 122
Stamford Hill, High Road 149
Stamford Hill, Rookwood Road (SF) 80
Stockwell (SW) .11, 12, 16, 17, 108
Stonebridge (SE) 12, 13, 61
Stratford (SD) 139
Stratford (Hackney) (H) 147
Streatham (AK) .5, 10, 13, 17, 63
Sutton (A) 110
Sutton (Carshalton) (CN) 13, 24

Thornton Heath (TH) 90
Tolworth (TR★) 123
Tottenham (AR) 82
Turnham Green (V) 10, 11, 13, 64
Twickenham (AB) 10, 19, 21, 65

Upton Park (U) 10, 139
Uxbridge (UX) 13, 97
Uxbridge (Wing's) (WS★) 156

Victoria, Gillingham Street (GM) 5, 7, 10, 11, 67
Victoria Basement, Gillingham Street (GB) 67

Walthamstow (WW) 21, 71
Walworth (WL) 19, 72, 153
Wandsworth (WD) 144
Waterloo (Red Arrow) (RA) 1, 6, 111
Wembley (WB★) 156
Westbourne Park (X) 13, 17, 18, 98
West Green (WG) 74
West Ham (WH) 21, 74
Willesden (AC) 10, 19, 129
Wood Green (WN) 83

Left and right:
Examples of garage codes
and running numbers on a
Connex Trident on route 60
and on a London United
Metrobus working from the
now-closed Kingston garage.
Author

Garages in order of LT/TfL garage code

Wood Lane (B)		123
A	Sutton	110
AB	Twickenham	10, 19, 21, 65
AC	Willesden	10, 19, 129
AD	Palmers Green	79
AE	Hendon	8, 37
AF	Putney	107
AG	Ash Grove	5, 17, 92, 153
AH	Nunhead	47
AH★	Brentford	145
AK	Streatham	5, 10, 13, 17, 63
AM	Plumstead	13, 51
AN★	Acton	94
AP	Seven Kings	10, 58
AR	Tottenham	82
AT	Acton	94
AV	Hounslow	3, 8, 15, 115
AW	Abbey Wood	9, 13, 21
B	Battersea (Hester Road)	19, 23, 153
B	Wood Lane	123
BA	Barking, Ripple Road	134
BA	Battersea, Hester Road Yard	86, 153
BB	Battersea (London General)	105
BC	Beddington Cross	146
BF	Beddington Farm	3, 7, 86, 145, 153
BN	Brixton	86
BT★	Edgware	146
BV	Belvedere	92
BW	Bow	134
BX	Bexleyheath	100
C	Athol Street, Poplar	22
CA	Clapham	26
CE	Colindale	12, 28
CF	Chalk Farm	25
CH	Chadwell Heath	136
CL	Clay Hall	27
CN	Carshalton	13, 24
CN★	Croydon, Beddington Farm	3, 7, 86, 145, 153
CT	Clapton	76
D	Dalston	7, 13, 20, 29
DA	Dagenham, Choats Road	147
DM	Dagenham, Chequers Lane	147
DR★	Old Kent Road	147
DX★	Barking, Ripple Road	76, 149
E	Enfield	77
EC★	Edmonton Wharf	77, 153
ED	Elmers End	16, 17, 31
EM	Edmonton	30
EM★	Edmonton Wharf	77, 153
EW	Edgware	5, 11, 18, 25
F	Putney Bridge	54
FW	Fulwell	5, 113, 145
FY	Finchley	32
G	Forest Gate	33
G	Greenford	96
GB	Victoria Basement	67
GM	Victoria	5, 7, 10, 11, 67

H	Hackney	13, 33
H	Hackney (Stratford)	147
HB	Hammersmith	12, 34
HD	Harrow Weald	127
HH	Hounslow Heath	117
HK★	Ash Grove (Hackney CT)	150
HL	Hanwell	36
HN★	Harlesden, Goodhall Street	154
HR	Harlesden, Atlas Road	127
HT	Holloway	130
HW	Southall	60
ID	Ilford	12, 40
IH	Isleworth	12, 15, 40
J	Holloway	37
K	Kingston	19, 117, 118
L	Loughton	5, 41
LB	Lea Bridge	12, 40
LW★	Southall	151
M	Mortlake	10, 11, 13, 19, 42
MB★	Orpington (Green Street Green)	153
MC★	Croydon, Redhouse Road and Beddington Lane	154
MH	Muswell Hill	21, 44
N	Norwood	13, 19, 89
NA	North Acton	131
NP	Northumberland Park	148, 149
NS	North Street, Romford	4, 5, 17, 138
NW	North Wembley	128
NX	New Cross	11, 103
OB	St Mary Cray, Nugent Industrial Estate	143
ON	Alperton	4, 10, 11, 17, 95
OR★	St Mary Cray, Faraday Way	96
P	Old Kent Road	7, 19, 49
PB	Potters Bar	8, 10, 131
PD	Plumstead	13, 143
PM	Peckham, Bull Yard	4, 11, 14, 17, 49
PM	Peckham, Copeland Road	104
PR	Poplar	52

Q	Camberwell	19, 101
QB★	Battersea, Silverthorne Road	146, 151
R	Hammersmith (Riverside)	10, 11, 12, 55
RA	Waterloo (Red Arrow)	1, 6, 111
RD	Hornchurch	4, 38
RI★	Harlesden, Atlas Road	127
RL	Rye Lane, Peckham	12, 58
S	Shepherds Bush	17, 119
SD	Stratford	139
SE	Stonebridge	12, 13, 61
SF	Stamford Hill, Rookwood Road	80
SO★	Harrow	155
SP	Sidcup	12, 59
SW	Stockwell	11, 12, 16, 17, 108
T	Leyton	136
TB	Bromley	141
TC	Croydon, Brighton Road	20, 88
TF★	Fulwell (Stanley Road - TGM)	155
TH	Thornton Heath	90
TL	Catford	142
TR★	Tolworth	123
U	Upton Park	10, 139
UX	Uxbridge	13, 97
V	Stamford Brook	10, 11, 122
V	Turnham Green	10, 11, 13, 64
W	Cricklewood	10, 19, 124
WB★	Wembley	156
WD	Wandsworth	144
WG	West Green	74
WH	West Ham	21, 74
WK	Hounslow Heath	117
WL	Walworth	19, 72, 153
WN	Wood Green	83
WS★	Uxbridge	156
WW	Walthamstow	21, 71
X	Middle Row	13, 42
X	Westbourne Park	13, 17, 18, 98
Y	St Mary Cray	96